The Gen Y Handbook

Praise for *The Gen Y Handbook*

"The next generation has changed the work equation as much as they have had the equation changed on them. New technologies, The Great Recession, and tuition inflation continue to reshape the promise of work and its realities. In *The GenY Handbook*, Diane Spiegel takes a practical approach to help managers, many of whom are personally unaffected by these changes, navigate and lead. She first creates an empathy for Generation Y and then suggests how managers should lead while they learn more about Millennials. Generation Y brings a unique relationship to technology with them to the work experience, along with a penchant for disregarding old rules and hierarchies.

Spiegel puts Generation Y into context without condescension or platitudes. In order for tomorrow's workforce to thrive, managers need a keen understanding of the realities they face, not the future they hope for. The future of the workplace should be constructive, not confrontational. With *The GenY Handbook* Spiegel creates a context for co-existence that will prove beneficial to Generation Y and to those who employ them."

Daniel W. Rasmus
Author, strategist, and industry analyst
Visit http://danielwrasmus.com "Put Your Future in Context"
Author of *Listening to the Future* and *Management by Design*

"Economic realities of the past several years may have frozen hiring and discouraged the retirement of older workers, but the issues of demographic change and leadership succession lurk just under the surface in many workplaces. As we drive deeper into the 2010s, organizations in every industry face mounting challenges of how to recruit, train, manage, and motivate next-generation talent. In *The GenY Handbook*, Diane Spiegel dispenses practical, common-sense advice for tapping into GenY's entrepreneurial spirit, collaborative work style, and affinity for digital technology, while respecting their unique generational experience and challenges. *The GenY Handbook* is a valuable addition to any manager's bookshelf."

Rob Salkowitz
Author of *Generation Blend: Managing Across the Technology Age Gap* and
*Young World Rising: How Youth, Technology and Entrepreneurship are
Changing the World from the Bottom Up*
http://robsalkowitz.com/

"The author has spent years looking across all the generations and has selected one for concentration in this book. She has given us a treasure. If your team is composed of even one member of this generation, you will love this book. The author provides research and experience-based tips and tools that will enable you to immediately improve your interaction and thereby impact business results.

Diane has written one of the best books I have seen on this subject. Her tips, charts, stories, case studies, and summaries make this immediately useful and applicable not only to the generation she concentrates on, but to your general communication with anyone on your team."

Beverly Kaye
Founder, Career Systems International
Author of *Up Is Not the Only Way: A Guide to Developing Workforce Talent*
Co-author of *Help Them Grow or Watch Them Go,*
Love 'em or Lose 'em, and *Love It, Don't Leave It*

"The *Gen Y Handbook* offers and delivers on how to engage and build effective relationships with this capable and tech-savvy, talented generation. The potentially positive impact that these young motivated employees impart is critical to long-term business success. Understanding what they are looking for and creating an environment that fosters innovation and creativity is key to working with Gen Y. Ms. Spiegel's book provides an easy to utilize continuum of content and is a must-read for managers and leaders as they navigate the ever-changing business backdrop."

Lisa Flesher
Vice President Human Resources, The Gap Inc.

"The impact of the Gen Ys has become a central focus, not just for professors but also for those who employ this generation around campus. *The Gen Y Handbook* is a great reference guide as more and more of this younger generation takes on even greater responsibility within our educational communities. We have many departments that have the four generations who work together. They often have misunderstanding about working hard versus working effectively, about workplace boundaries, and about what are, and what are not, appropriate work habits. I highly recommend Diane Spiegel's book as we look at employee productivity, engagement, retention, and effective coaching."

Prany Sananikone
Director of Diversity Relations & Educational Programs
Office of Equal Opportunity & Diversity
University of California, Irvine

The Gen Y Handbook

✧ ✧ ✧ ✧ ✧

*Applying Relationship Leadership
to Engage Millennials*

Diane E. Spiegel

SelectBooks, Inc.

New York

This edition published by SelectBooks, Inc.

For information address SelectBooks, Inc., New York, New York.

First Edition

ISBN 978-1-59079-956-7

Library of Congress Cataloging-in-Publication Data

Spiegel, Diane E.
The gen Y handbook : applying relationship leadership to engage
millennials / Diane E. Spiegel. – First Edition.
     pages cm
Includes bibliographical references.
Summary: "Head of a corporate training business examines issues of
Generation Y entering the workforce, including their conflicts with Baby
Boomer managers who have different work ethics. She describes the Gen Y
mindset to help company owners understand their distinct values and talents
and recommends the right methods of leadership to motivate the Millennials
to achieve their full potential"–Provided by publisher.
ISBN 978-1-59079-956-7 (pbk. : alk. paper)
1. Generation Y. 2. Work ethic. 3. Leadership. 4. Communication in
management. I. Title. HQ799.5.S65 2013
305.23—dc23
                          2012031244

Manufactured in the United States of America

10 9 8 7 6 5 4 3 2 1

To the smart, inspiring Millennials,
including my children Marc and Victoria,
who fill me with optimism for the future
as this generation takes flight.

To my soul mate and husband Steve,
thank you for the encouragement and support!

Contents

Acknowledgments

Books are collaborative processes that begin with an idea, but need much nurturing, vision, and support and this journey became real when William Gladstone at Waterside Productions said yes! His wisdom in partnering with SelectBooks has been terrific and the team's ideas and suggestions have been valued and appreciated.

In the research and planning of the book, Prany Sananik, Director of Diversity Relations and Educational Programs at University California, Irvine, has been inspirational, supportive, and informative. His willingness to share and his access to his team and colleagues have been most generous and appreciated.

I want to express appreciation to all the client companies, too numerous to list, who helped with focus groups, access to research, and sharing their perspectives. The time, effort, and results will help supervisors and managers better engage the many Millennials who are in today's workforce, wanting to do a great job, but not always understanding how to connect. Your contributions have opened many new avenues of dialogue.

I also owe a great deal to all the hundreds of Gen Ys interviewed both in person and online, who shared their insights, viewpoints, and hope for the future. One of the key focus areas was on the prevalence and meaning of tattoos which provided amazing insights into these talented twenty-something's creativity, thoughtfulness, and depth.

Finally, to my colleagues and friends who were encouraging and ever supportive—thanks for coming along on this voyage.

Introduction

Our perception of the world is filtered through the lens of our values and assumptions, some of which are formed soon after we are born, while others develop later through the influence of our families, communities, and socioeconomic and cultural experiences. In this handbook we move beyond stereotypes or easy categorization to address the unique characteristics, impact, and work potential of Generation Y (or, as they are often referred to, the Millennials) as they enter the workforce.

Much has been written about these 75 million[1] tech-savvy, multi-tasking Americans, born from (approximately) 1981 through 1999 who make up one-third of the population in the United States and will soon make up a majority of the workforce.[2] The term "Gen Y" first appeared in an August 1993 editorial in *Ad Age* to describe the teenagers of the day, then aged twelve or younger, as the cohort following Gen X.

Generation X is frequently defined as those born between 1965 and 1980, and were so-named by photographer Robert Capa for the undefined and uncertain future they were facing. Having been raised with computer skills and shaped by the Internet for much of their lives, these technology natives have a distinct familiarity with the information tools that have changed the way business is conducted and the way people communicate.

Due to the connectivity that the web offers, and because they understand how to maximize technology and social media's impact, Generation Y, or the "Millennial" Generation, see themselves as "global citizens," part of a worldwide community. The children who are part of Generation Y have also been called the "Trophy Kids" and "Echo Boomers" when they are offspring of Baby Boomers,[3] the large generation following World War II. Whether Millennials have young "Gen X" parents or older "Baby Boomer" parents, many have been brought up in families that have been involved in every aspect of their lives—running interference, scheduling lessons, coaching sports, taking them to group activities, helping with schoolwork and college applications, and coaching them on career and job options. These factors influence how Millennial employees approach work, how they identify with work, and even how they perceive the traditional employee/employer relationship.

This book will help you understand WHY Millennials come to the workplace with different ideas about how work is accomplished, and is filled with many HOW TOs to help you understand behaviors that might seem different from when you first began your career. Many people on your team, or those whose work output you are responsible for, may not be employees but contractors or consultants. Understanding how to manage, motivate, and lead these young workers is a key not only to your success but to making the process of accomplishing work a less stressful, more enjoyable experience.

As this generation was growing up, their parents played an influential and unusually collaborative role in their lives. A focused parental involvement is not a new concept, but the mindset of this generation's parents was clearly announced by the prevalent "Baby on Board" signs taped to the windows of their cars as they transported their precious cargo. This was a foreshadowing of things to come—a generation whose parents were emotionally invested in raising not only well-cared for, smart, and capable kids, but ones equipped to compete in the growing tech backdrop of today's business. Parents coached and guided their kids to build their resumes for success by attending workshops, summer camps, and engaging in volunteer activities. They often even paid for them to have their own coaches, whether it was to teach them to increase soccer skills or to learn another language.

Often referred to as "entitled," Millennials don't view themselves as such; they feel "deserving" based on their experiences of what they know and what they have been told. To allow you to visualize this difference, imagine what it would feel like if you had been raised by parents whose primary job was to protect you, consistently praise you, provide you with rewards (yes, even for just participating!), and you were in an environment which made you feel like the world revolved around you—are you feeling the YOU focus? Throughout the book, you will be asked to look through the Millennial lens and view the world through their perspectives.

As a corporate educator and facilitator, I've experienced the impact that multigenerational employment has had in the workforce. Much of the feedback I've obtained from conversations with company executives and discussions in our workshops is about the need for coaching for the development of employees of the younger generations. A common remark from executives is: "Why can't we find people like *us* to work in our company!" The sentiment being expressed is that they want employees like them who are willing to work sixty hours a week and put the job first, life second. Because 75 percent of America's Fortune 500 companies' CEOs are baby boomers, this mindset is prevalent. The pushback from both Gen Y and Gen Xers, however, has been consistent—they both want balance in their work and life.

Both Gen X and Gen Y experienced their parents' "work ethic" and the return on their parents' investment in their work, which often failed to pay off as the company they were employed by filed for bankruptcy, was downsized, or became obsolete. This left a tremendous impression. Coupled with the amazing efficiencies that can be obtained with technologies, such as Skype, video conferencing, and sharing computer screens, this shifted the perspective that work had to be done on-site, at a company's headquarters.

"Relationship leadership" is a key theme utilized throughout the Gen Y Handbook and is a recommended leadership approach to managing Generation Y employees. Relationship leadership is a collaborative style of leadership where trust is at the core as opposed to the traditional "top-down" or command and control style that implies you are only on a "need-to-know" basis with the employees. Command and control is often found in companies with a defined hierarchy management style whose effectiveness is being questioned in this highly information-rich era.

Relationship leadership focuses on having positive relationships and a sense of community in the business organization by supporting and developing team members and, ultimately, by empowering people. This model of management leadership works best for a generation that looks for a connection to how they fit into a company. They want to understand the impact of what they contribute, how *what* the company does affects others, how what the company does impacts communities (whether that is a direct contribution, such as in the jobs and opportunities offered), and how this relates to those who lead and direct their work.

Each chapter represents a dimension of developing effective business relationships with the Gen Ys you lead and manage. Sprinkled throughout the chapters are also "Millennial Minutes." These are brief nuggets of information that take a minute or so to think about and help provide short and easy ideas about how to engage Millennials with a new awareness of what the Millennial generation is all about. Case studies are also utilized to provide real-world scenarios and conversations that will provide examples of what to say and how to respond in the most common situations that supervisors and managers have shared with us in our focus groups as well as in workshops. Additionally, there is information from a diversity of companies about how they are making adjustments and changes to maximize young talent.

Chapter one, "Gaining Insight into Gen Y," discusses how this young generation tends to redefine workplace boundaries and how this changes expectations and assumptions, especially in the area of workplace transparency. Understanding their values about wanting to be able to see through processes and systems is essential to having successful relationships with Millennials. Having clarity about the "rubric" measurements they grew up with that define what great work is, as compared to good work or even acceptable work, will help you to move forward in building effective business relationships with them.

Chapter two, "Understanding Gen Y Potential," helps to demystify some striking differences from previous generations including the prevalence of tattoos and explains how understanding this creative canvas supports relationship-building. Since "entitlement" has been a word consistently used to describe the attitude Millennials bring with them, this chapter explains why this perception of Gen Y is rampant and what being entitled means to them. Ways to talk to someone who appears entitled are suggested in order to prevent stymying communication and the building of a sound working relationship. Additional ways to mine their potential are reviewed which include the use of partner mentoring along with having clarity about what motivates Millennials.

Chapter three, "What Trust Means to Gen Ys," provides the foundation for developing strong and effective business relationships by defining what trust in the workplace means, sharing ways to improve workplace trust, and highlighting how collaboration outperforms the traditional command and control styles of leading.

Chapter four, "Helping Gen Ys to Develop Acumen," underscores how ongoing coaching improves performance as well as improving communication that directly impacts Gen Y's work dedication or work ethic. Cultivating acumen improves professionalism by helping you achieve your department or organization's business goals with less internal resistance.

Chapter five, "Supporting Gen Ys to Find Their Passion," directs your coaching and employee guidance to tap into the vast resources, ideas, and talents that Millennials want to share and to contribute as quickly as they can. As we highlight in this chapter, social media has changed the way business is conducted and the way we communicate. Millennials are the first generation to be digital natives. It's as if they come "pre-wired," and it's to your advantage to tap in and find where they can contribute and connect.

Chapter six, "Building Relationships with Gen Ys," provides ways to show appreciation and how to continue to build business relationships, using the RIGHT model to improve your ability to engage and lead. This chapter also explains how to repair a broken relationship. This can easily happen when Millennials are overly comfortable blogging and sharing on various social media sites how they feel about their work and their boss.

Chapter seven, "How to Interview and Onboard Gen Y Talent," supports a new perspective on things such as the "tell all" resumes that Millennials provide. Suggestions are given about how to interview and successfully orient these young people and there is a strong emphasis on how your organization will be well served by being Millennial-friendly!

This book has a multipurpose design. You can read cover to cover, or you can go directly to a specific chapter's content in order to utilize the information that best suits your needs. My intent is to help you better connect, communicate, and understand the best ways to increase engagement and efficiency at work. Building effective business relationships can help you make your work environment more productive, thereby benefiting all.

Generational differences in the workplace is not a new topic. In 1950 Karl Mannheim, who was considered to be the grandfather of generational research, defined a generation as a group of individuals similar in age whose members have experienced noteworthy events within a set period of time. According to Mannheim's sociological theory, when a group of people share a common birth period, they are cemented by the significant events and social changes of that era. The events become a part of an individual's identity and influence that person's views on the world, but they also impact the attitudes, beliefs, and perceptions of all persons born in that period to create a collective generational perspective.

Descriptions of Today's Four Generations in the Workplace

(Please note that the date parameters for defining generations varies according to researchers, so the number of people given for each generation may be different in other sources and books about the generations.)

Generation	Characteristics	Why are they this way?	How many?
Traditionalist 1925–1945[1]	Patriotic Hardworking Respectful of authority Obeys chain of command Self-sacrificing Defers gratification[2]	Having grown up during wartime, patriotism was expected, orders from authority figures were followed, and if personal sacrifice was necessary, it was done without complaint.	75 million 10 million still in the workplace[2]
Baby Boomers 1946–1964[3]	Optimistic Idealistic Believe anything is possible Agents of social change Hard work is their badge of honor.[4]	As the children of so many veterans, they wanted to change the status quo, imagining a world of equality and peace.	80 million In 2011, the oldest of the Boomers, age sixty-five, became eligible for Social Security and Medicare benefits.[4]
Generation X 1965–1980[5]	Skeptical of others Depend on themselves Suspicious of authority Free-agent mindsets Priority on family[6,7]	The divorce rate was 50 percent so many kids grew up in single parent homes and became known as the "latch key" generation.	46 Million The 2011 publication "The Generation X Report," based on annual surveys used in the Longitudinal Study of adults, found this generation to be highly educated, active, balanced, happy, and family-oriented.[6]
Generation Y (or Millennials) 1981–1999[7]	Flexible Technology natives Global Citizens Well-connected Need daily feedback Expect transparency[8,9,10]	Grew up in child-centric homes with high expectations; the Internet was part of their orientation from birth.	75 million They make up one-third of the United States population.[8]

1 http://www.valueoptions.com/spotlight_YIW/traditional.htm.
2 http://en.wikipedia.org/wiki/Silent_Generation.
3 http://en.wikipedia.org/wiki/Baby_boomers.
4 http://www.metlife.com/assets/cao/mmi/publications/Profiles/mmi-middle-boomer-demographic-profile.pdf.
5 http://en.wikipedia.org/wiki/Gen_x.
6 http://www.metlife.com/assets/cao/mmi/publications/Profiles/mmi-gen-x-demo-graphic-profile.pdf.
7 Dr. Joanne Sujansky and Dr. Jan Ferri-Reed, *Keeping the Millennials: Why Companies are Losing Billions in Turnover to This Generation and What to Do about It* (John Wiley & Sons, 2009), 79–80.

Defining Moments for the current generations include:

- TRADITIONALIST 1900–1945
  World War II
  The Great Depression
  Korean War

- BABY BOOMERS 1946–1964
  Election and assassination of John F. Kennedy
  Cuban missile crisis
  Civil rights movement
  Women's movement
  Walk on the moon
  Vietnam War
  Woodstock

- GENERATION X 1965–1980
  Challenger disaster
  Fall of the Berlin Wall
  AIDS
  Sesame Street
  MTV

- MILLENNIALS or GENERATION Y 1981–1999
  Murrah Federal Building bombing in Oklahoma City
  Columbine High School shooting
  September 11, 2001

This list of defining moments is not intended to be comprehensive, but to provide a flavor of how significant events impact a collective generation. Who we are and how we perceive the world is based on a host of circumstances beyond our generational experiences, including where we were born and raised, who we were raised by, our birth order, heritage, race, religion, cultural and normative beliefs, and economic circumstances.

Footnotes for Generation chart continued:
8 Rob Salkowitz, *Generation Blend: Managing Across the Technology Age Gap* (John Wiley & Sons, Inc. 2008), 1–15.
9 Kit Yarrow and Jayne O'Donnell, *Gen Buy: How Tweens, Teens and Twenty-Somethings are Revolutionizing Retail* (Jossey-Bass, 2009), 1–19.
  9http://www.metlife.com/assets/cao/mmi/publications/Profiles/mmi-gen-y-demographic-profile.pdf.
10 Rob Salkowitz, *Generation Blend: Managing Across the Technology Age Gap* (John Wiley & Sons, Inc. 2008), 1–15.

As you read through the chapters, it's important to remember that the intent is not to stereotype a generation, but to utilize the lens through which we perceive a collective generation's experiences as you make sense of what Millennial talent can bring to the workplace and how to best harness and apply their talent, skill, creativity, and ideas.

Managing Gen Ys by using the mottos for the way in which you were managed, such as "DO UNTO OTHERS ..." will not allow you to obtain the results you are after. To move forward, you need to first assess who you are leading and where they are in terms of business performance. Then determine HOW they might benefit from a different approach to being supervised so you can have highly engaged, motivated, innovative, and committed team players. Ask them: "How do you want to be led? How do you want to be coached?"

Here's wishing you good luck on your journey as you engage and lead the Millennials on your team!

The Gen Y Handbook

✦ 1 ✦

Gaining INSIGHT into Gen Ys

*INSIGHT: the ability to see clearly and intuitively into
the nature of a complex person, situation, or subject.*

Every generation brings its collective experiences, complexities, and
expectations to the workplace. I'm often asked, "Is Generation Y really
so unique and different? Doesn't every new generation bring their own
set of values and expectations?" The answer is yes, and yes! Millennials
are unique in that they are the first generation of digital natives;
they've grown up with not only the computer but the Internet and
everything that these circumstances entail. Their social networking
skills connect them with others who can quickly provide information,
help solve problems, and make suggestions. This generation's tech
savvy has also connected them to many places around the planet to
enable them to view themselves as Global Citizens.

This contributes to the interesting phenomenon that Generation Y
has far fewer boundaries between each other and all other people than
previous generations at their age. And the customary cultural boundaries pertaining to dress, language, conduct, and social interactions
have all rapidly shifted for this generation.

During workshops I hear from many participants who, although
they agree that Millennials are smart, think they lack common sense
and sometimes need assistance connecting the dots. Part of this challenge is that they have been educated to collaborate and work on
teams—a good attribute, but challenging if they are asked to work
independently. In a significant shift in values, they also do not identify
with the concept that you first need to "pay your dues" before you can
advance at work, and this can cause conflict with the values of their
Baby Boomer and Generation X managers.

A remarkable characteristic is that over 50 percent of this generation currently in the workplace volunteered during high school to support a number of diverse causes in their communities. Though volunteering was a requirement in some high schools and was needed to get into some of the more prestigious colleges, Millennials discovered that giving back to their communities was enriching. This desire to give back is a wonderful starting point for employers to develop corporate philanthropic processes within the appropriate boundaries of the employer, and a natural fit for corporate social responsibility (CSR). Giving back comes naturally to them and discovering ways for your Millennial employees to support community charities is a win-win approach to further connect them to the company as well as the community.

Generation Y is also referred to as Gen WHY? This generation has a great curiosity and needs to understand why decisions are made, why you asked them to do something a particular way, and why something is given priority. This concept is further explored in this chapter, especially in the discussion about boundaries. Previous generations did not always feel empowered to ask *why* when an assignment or task was delegated, or felt they had a reason to know. They did as they were told, whether they thought it was a good idea or not.

As you work through this chapter and gain insights into the values and habits of the Millennials on your team, it will help you to connect and communicate with them. Also reviewed in this section are expectations and assumptions which are key to understanding why this generation may come to work with a different approach than yours. The case study provided allows you a first-hand look into how you can manage and direct a conversation that builds relationships without compromising your standards.

The Millennial Minute below, as well as all the Millennial Minutes throughout the book, provide further tips and ideas to support building effective relationships to help you engage and lead.

Redefining Workplace Boundaries

In previous generations, boundaries were clearly defined. There were boundaries for every aspect of life: how we spent our time, our social behavior, work behavior, communication, attire, and our technological capabilities. How this generation thinks about "time" is very different; what is considered really "old" by this generation could be a three-year-old cell phone!

🕐 *MILLENNIAL MINUTE*

> Since Generation Y feels strongly about giving back to the community and supporting philanthropic causes, take every opportunity, such as meetings, blogs, and department communications, to share with them how your company is contributing to the community as well as showcasing how your company is being a socially responsible corporate citizen.

◦ ◦ ◦ ◦ ◦ ◦ ◦ ◦ ◦ ◦ ◦ ◦ ◦ ◦ ◦ ◦

In previous generations the time of day when you called someone at home had boundaries: not too early, not during dinner, and typically not after 10:00 p.m. There were numerous social boundaries, such as how you addressed someone older than you or how young men came to the door to meet their date's parents. There were also appropriate places to take your date and curfews to be obeyed.

Work was attended "from and to" specific hours, and the items brought home in one's briefcase were reviewed in the evening. There were "work clothes" (whether that was a suit and tie or a uniform), "play clothes," and Sunday or "dress-up" clothes. The attire to be worn to work was clear: no "business casual" interpretation required!

The work world was based on the military model of rank and file. Defined hierarchy and command and control were the norm. You knew where you stood in the company's "food chain," who you could talk to, and who needed to be addressed as Mr. or Mrs. You knew you had to put in your time before climbing the ladder of success, and like competing in a triathlon, you had to complete each event before moving to the next.

How long tasks take to accomplish has dramatically changed, too. Research and data gathering once took a long time; now it can take seconds with the right Internet hook-up and a good search engine. While research about Generation Y was being conducted, many executives shared their frustration with the challenge posed by trying to find someone willing to work sixty to seventy hours per week, as they did. These executives just couldn't understand why the idea of paying your dues, as they did, was being rejected. The Gen Ys, on the other hand, are sorry that it takes *you* so long to get your work done!

Boundaries have changed significantly throughout society as well as in the workplace. Millennials have lived through several of the most dynamic decades of change. They are the first global generation, and this global reach has resulted in the enormity of the ensuing boundary changes to which we have been a witness. Gen X voiced concerns about work–life balance, but Generation Y is almost twice the population of Gen X so their workplace impact is more profound, especially in regard to this topic. As children and young people, baby boomers were to be "seen and not heard," their boundaries with others were clearly defined (respect your elders, don't talk back to adults, never use profanity in "mixed company"), and their parents, relatives, and other adults would provide feedback if they were not behaving within those confines.

Much has been written about the Millennials as the "Trophy Kids, the pride and joy of their dedicated parents." In 2008 Ron Alsop, long-time reporter and editor of *The Wall Street Journal,* was one of the first to write about their large impact in his book, *The Trophy Kids Grow Up: How the Millennial Generation is Shaking Up the Workplace.* In only a few years they will make up the majority of the workforce. Employers have no choice except to modify business culture to accommodate their high expectations and demands for freedom, ongoing communication, and flexibility.

The "best friend" parenting style has been a common experience among members of Generation Y. This style has changed the traditional boundaries between parents and children, resulting in a high degree of parental involvement in their lives beyond college and into the workplace. In a recent online survey, Millennials shared the information that 75 percent of the time they consulted their parents before making any big employment decisions. They claimed they often view their parents as their "best friends"—a significant change from the relationship Baby Boomers had with their "square" Traditionalist parents. (In the 1960s a "square" referred to someone who clung to repressive, traditional, stereotypical, one-sided, or "in the box" ways of thinking.)

Gen Ys arrive in the workplace without a "boundaries" frame of mind. They believe, as they have been told all their lives, that they are smart, educated, and important, and that they have much to contribute. From a leadership perspective, we often think these "kids" have no respect for their elders. But they are only reflecting how they have been raised: they were taught to ask questions without regard for people's status and to be inclusive of others. They tend to feel that they have every right to talk to the president, CEO, or any executive, even if they have been working only a short time. Are they expecting their supervisor to also have the loving "best friend" PARENTS style they have been raised with? Yes! That's been their model, and they are comfortable with this and know how to respond to it. According to Millennials, the ideal boss would be:

- ✓ **Flexible** (About work schedules, boundaries about proper work attire, management of their time, and methods and processes used to accomplish the work.)

- ✓ **Respectful of their ideas** (Millennials don't respect titles; they respect people.)

- ✓ **Understanding** (They want managers to hear them out and try not to dismiss them out of hand.)

- ✓ **Have strong communication skills** (Gen Ys need to know what is occurring. They deal well with the truth. When you level with them and provide clear reasons and rationale, they know how to manage that data. They do not do well when they don't have information—there is too much ambiguity.)

- ✓ **Easy to get along with** (But don't think "easygoing" means reducing standards or expectations. Millennials just don't want the "we–they" syndrome. *Can't we just get along?*)

- ✓ **Caring** (You know you are not their parents, and you may or may not really care—but showing some interest and concern will take you much further in obtaining the kind of output and efficiency your Millennials can deliver.)

Generation Y believes that work should be enjoyable. This is a different perspective from Traditionalists and Baby Boomers, who believe that *work* should be just that! Since many Millennials know that their parents will continue to provide support (75 percent of twentysomethings still get some financial support from their parents), they have a safety net which allows them to leave a job they do not like. Even in these challenging economic times, 50 percent of those who responded to a recent survey said they would leave a job they "hated," even if they did not have another one lined up.[4]

Gen Ys also have a different perspective when it comes to boundaries about sharing information and feelings. Since they have grown up with all things digital they are comfortable finding and giving information.

They believe that they are entitled and welcomed to share the events of their lives with anyone. The current top-five social media sites include Facebook, Twitter, LinkedIn, MySpace, and Google+, and this is where many Millennials share things in common. Four in ten surveyed responded that they have a personal profile on MySpace or Facebook. It is not unusual to find extensive blogs about what they are doing, their thoughts and feelings, and many of the mundane facts of their everyday lives. This sharing of information has no boundaries. The content of this information has no boundaries. If you arrived at someone's personal home page from a different planet and were trying to understand what it all meant, you might first observe what appears to be a high level of narcissism.

We're seeing a unique phenomenon in the workplace: a reverse accumulation of knowledge. That is, the younger you are, the more likely you are to know about technology. This is the first time in history that younger employees come to the workplace with more knowledge about how things work than those that have been there before them.

The implications of this are profound. Since Generation Y offspring have been the ones with the ability to offer "tech support" to their parents, they grew up providing that technological aptitude, filling in where their parents' information was insufficient. This sent a clear message: you are important, your voice matters, and what you have to say adds value. Being asked to sit at the "kids' table" did not usually apply, so they bring this participative mindset to the workplace. In addition, the older norm of children being seen and not heard did not apply to them, yet many in the workplace use this perspective to evaluate employee behaviors.

🕐 MILLENNIAL MINUTE

Since members of Generation Y are perceived by many as less mature than those from previous generations were at the same age, providing specific feedback about workplace boundaries serves everyone well. Once you let go of the "when I was your age" paradigm and tap into the many talents and skills Gen Ys bring to the workplace, you will begin to feel less frustrated. This is not the same work environment in which you started your career. Would you really want to go back, say, thirty years and give up your Internet connection, your Blackberry, your personal computer, and your iPod?

• • • • • • • • • • • • • • • • • • • •

As these boundaries have shifted, Millennials have brought a new set of expectations. This may require you, as their supervisor, to modify a few things. A good place to begin is to be clear in your mind about the behavior limits in your area—whether that is about attire, language, demeanor, or the way work is accomplished. A quality conversation about these boundaries with specific information presented in a collaborative fashion is a great place to begin. The effort will be rewarded!

Expectations and Assumptions

Although Millennials are early technology adopters, because they are maturing more slowly than generations before them, they come to the workplace with their own expectations. When they come to work, many bring the expectation that, like their hovering "helicopter parents," you as their supervisor are there to help them, coach them, guide them, and provide a lot of feedback.

For maximum performance, it's essential to understand what they expect from the beginning, and to be able to manage their assumptions balanced with your own expectations. Being able to come to work in flip-flops and ripped jeans, and listen to their iPods while working, is their expectation. If this does not fit into your workplace protocol, be clear and specific. You may get some pushback but remember, they have been brought up to ask questions and to *question*. They have been part of the learning process, not just participators. This can become an advantage once you have clarified what's expected and provide feedback as needed.

Most companies do not have any written policies about cell phone use at the office. Most people accept their personal phone calls, texts, and email alongside their workload. Millennials are accustomed to texting all day long. They do not typically see 8:00 to 5:00 as being exclusively for work. Instead they see it as part of the seamless, integrated process customary in their lives. You do your work, check your messages, respond, and keep on working. If your company or department has a policy about cell phone usage, be sure it is understood. The work/personal boundary can be unclear for Millennials because they have experienced a format in which everything is connected.

Because most Millennials talk, text, or email their parents daily, adolescence is prolonged. Being a "tethered generation" allows them to try out different jobs and careers. According to Pew Research Center they want to get married, but postpone the time for this. (Only 20 percent of Gen Ys aged 18 to 29 are married compared to 40 percent of Baby Boomers and 30 percent of Gen X at their age.) Because they are waiting until their late twenties or early thirties to marry and have kids, the number of options available to them has dramatically increased.[5] This prolonged adolescence is their form of "Adultescence"[6] —the seemingly endless stretch of time between prom night and confident adult self-sufficiency.

Generation Y worked in groups and teams while growing up. This occurred in schools, on sports teams, and in the many community activities they were committed to. They are very comfortable with team input and feedback from coaches. They have grown up believing that a coach's job was to help them improve their game in every way.

Millennials have grown up with this model of "talking to the authority figure"—whether this is a teacher, principal, coach, or college admissions counselor. This is their frame of reference. The challenge, as their supervisor, is to meet them in a place that helps them understand what you expect without necessitating your transformation into a helicopter supervisor.

Parents are considered "trusted advisors," and Millennials consult with them about all key decisions. Even some of the minor decisions are a point of discussion. The impact of this mindset has been apparent in the workplace, with Millennials struggling to make the "right decision" when working independently. One of the opportunities you can take as their supervisor is to give them latitude about making small, independent decisions so they can become more comfortable with decision-making. Though this generation is well informed, tech savvy, and socially connected, they have been sheltered and, as a result, frequently lack the "street smarts" that previous generations brought to the workplace.

🕐 MILLENNIAL MINUTE

Gen Ys have learned much of what they know by doing it rather than by reading about it in a manual. In the competitive world of video games and online role-playing games, Millennials had great incentive to acquire intricate, difficult, or nearly impossible skills and to learn quickly through intuition or trial and error. They have no fear of trying new things when you provide empowerment and the opportunity.

• • • • • • • • • • • • • • • • • • •

Questions to Ask Gen Ys about Boundaries

By definition, conversations and coaching are intended to be a two-way process. The following questions are offered to help you connect and begin a meaningful conversation about boundaries:

What do you believe your job duties are, day-to-day?

Take this opportunity to understand, from their perspective, what they *believe* their daily responsibilities are and provide any course correction. Keep in mind that clear boundaries may not exist in their frame of reference.

What is your definition of "business casual"?

Provide clear and specific feedback if their definition of business casual does not fit yours. Remember, they are getting many of their ideas about these things from other Millennials.

Why is it important to our business for you to be at work "on time"?

Share WHY it is important to their job to be on time to work and back from lunch promptly. Make no assumptions that they understand they should be on time, as they may think it's just some random rule you use to control them! When you share sound business reasons, you are providing the *why* that will encourage them to comply.

What are some things you are skilled or proficient at that you have not yet been able to apply to your job?

Millennials believe that they are underutilized in their jobs and if their bosses knew what they could do, they would be able to contribute at a much higher level. Listen in earnest—perhaps they can!

What is your understanding of when it is appropriate to text and email during work?

Many companies have clear policies about this that are shared during new-hire training. If your policy is vague, provide the guidelines. Work and non-work activities are blurred for many Millennials, so you will benefit from clarifying.

✳ *Case Study*

Jody is a baby boomer manager and is very direct and not keen on the idea that this generation doesn't want to "pay their dues" because she has certainly had to be patient and pay hers! Jody has worked hard to get where she is and believes we all must earn our place in an organization. Due to a recent merger, Jody now has a new go-getter Millennial on her team. Adam is smart, talented on the tech side, and very good with people. Adam believes he is the most qualified to lead the new task force. Jody does not want to dampen his spirits, but she knows he's not ready to lead this assignment. She does think that, with some training and coaching, he holds a lot of potential. Here's their conversation as Jody shares with Adam why he is not "entitled" to this opportunity and how he can become ready to take on more responsibility. Adam asked for the face-to-face meeting, as his needs (in this case, wanting to lead the task force) are usually of an urgent nature!

Adam: *Thanks for meeting me. I know you've been really busy, but I feel like you are not taking me seriously and I know you have not known me very long—but I'm really dedicated to what I do.*

Jody: *I appreciate your enthusiasm and your ability to be persuasive can be charming, but you haven't worked with our team long enough for us to feel comfortable with you taking a leadership role on this task force.*

Adam: *What do you mean? You just said you hardly know me. How do you know I'm not ready?*

Jody: *This task force is high profile and leading this group will be challenging. What experience have you had doing this before? And what were your results?*

Adam: *Well, I've led lots of teams. I was president of my fraternity and chaired the United Way drive for our division.*

Jody: *That's a good start, but what experiences have you had in managing team conflict, dealing with egos without offending people, and making sure the task force is on point and meets its goals?*

Adam: *Well, I have had to deal with egos, but it was not always as successful as I would have liked.*

Jody: *This will be a good learning experience and in order to get the most out of this, take some notes during the next two focus group meetings and analyze what is said and done to keep those egos in check without* *derailing the meeting. Let's connect again after that and we will talk about your observations and how they can help you as you move forward.*

Adam: *Okay, that sounds like a good plan. I'm holding you to that follow-up meeting—so, no blowing me off!*

Jody: *I know you'll hold me to it!*

So What Transpired Here?

Because Jody took a few minutes to have a meaningful conversation with Adam, he has clarity about why he was not considered to lead this assignment, a game plan for how he can gain a better understanding of the skills needed, and the opportunity to come back to Jody to discuss and review. Millennials respond favorably to this type of coaching, especially when explained clearly with business reason and logic. Adam is now accountable for observing, learning, and sharing. These several minutes of dialogue were a great investment of Jody's time.

⏱ MILLENNIAL MINUTE

The first channel of filtering that often occurs for Gen Ys is "What's in It for Me?" (WIIFM) Lead with this concept when assigning work. How will it benefit them? How will it help their skill set? How will it make them more effective? How does the successful completion of this assignment lead to other job-enriching assignments? When you can add the WIIFM aspect as part of your conversation, it will encourage their participation and agreement, creating a stronger connection.

●　●　●　●　●　●　●　●　●　●　●　●　●　●　●　●　●　●

Meet the Helicopter and Lawnmower Parents!

"Helicopter parent" is a term for a parent who pays extremely close attention to his or her offspring's experiences and problems, particularly in regard to education and educational choices. These parents try to prevent any harm or failure from impacting their kids. They are so-named because, like helicopters, they hover closely overhead, rarely out of reach, whether their kids need them or not. An extension of this term has been coined for those who cross the line from a mere excess of zeal to unethical behavior, such as writing their children's college admission essays: "Black Hawk parents." (The reference is to the military helicopter of the same name.)

Some college professors are now referring to "Lawnmower Parents" to describe parents who attempt to smooth out and mow down all obstacles for their children. The impact of these hovering parenting styles has been felt in a number of different ways in the workplace. Helicopter parents now help write résumés and cover letters, provide coaching for the interview, and increasingly call potential employers with questions or concerns. ("Why didn't you call my amazing, brilliant, gifted child back?")

Sometimes these Lawnmower Parents try to interfere in their kids' workplaces regarding salaries and promotions, even when their children have graduated from college and are living on their own as adults. Parents may even call the human resource department of their children's employers to try to find out why their son or daughter received a particular rating on their performance appraisal, why they were passed over for promotion, why they were put on corrective warning. These actions seem like bold boundary crossings. If you have never experienced these phenomena, you might be wondering if this is being made up; it is not! Human resource professionals continue to be amazed by parents who cross these boundaries and try to intervene and advocate for their "child," even though their darling is twenty-something!

⏰ MILLENNIAL MINUTE

Many Helicopter Parents are baby boomers. Is it possible that in their quest to stay youthful, boomer parents really don't want their kids to grow up because *they* will be viewed as older? (Can you hear Bob Dylan singing "Forever Young"?)

• • • • • • • • • • • • • • • • • • •

The good news is that when an employee or prospective employee is an adult—that is, at least eighteen years old—employers are not authorized to speak to their parents. The bad news is that so many parents have such extensive influence over their Millennials (more so than previous generations at the same age) that alienating parents could be a poor choice. Companies with large numbers of Generation Y employees in their ranks are electing to have "Family Days" where they invite the family to tour the company, see where their Millennial is working, and hold workshops about benefits and retirement. Some companies have even taken it a step further by inviting these visiting parents to be part of focus groups related to their particular products. This is a great example of taking lemons and making lemonade!

Transparency in the Workplace

Transparency by definition means open, allowing light to pass through, clearly recognizable as what he or she really is. In Latin it means "shining through." Transparency in business means the open disclosure of certain policies; for example, why a company goes in a particular direction. Transparency implies openness, communication, and accountability. It is a metaphorical extension of the meaning used in the physical sciences: a "transparent" object is one that can be seen through.

Why is transparency so important? Employees and contractors, especially Millennials, want to know that what you claim is true and accurate. You can establish a sense of trust up front by being transparent.

For a business to be transparent certain rules need to be followed or guidelines put in place to keep us on track. After all, if a business pulls one way in regard to openness, communication, and accountability one day and another the next, clients will start to complain and eventually take their business elsewhere. Transparency matters in the business world today because your customers and employees know a lot about you and your business. There is far greater access to information and information sharing can occur at wildfire speed. Customers want to know that the quality of goods or services you provide are what you claim, and they want to know what resources are being used to develop and manufacture these goods.

When open communication and accountability exist in the company's culture, others will value your honesty and be drawn to you. There are many benefits to becoming a more transparent manager. When you share and answer questions honestly and directly, you become known as a leader who is trustworthy—because of this transparency. No one is asking you to be someone other than who you are, but to better connect with your Millennials, some style accommodations to become more transparent will serve you well!

Transparency as a management practice can be challenging. From a privacy and proprietary perspective, some things should not be shared. But there are opportunities to share the things which can help your

Millennials understand how the business works and the methods and processes which allow customers and clients to see into an organization. The following are ideas to help you as you become more transparent:

Be honest—Millennials appreciate "no BS" conversations. If information can't be shared, tell them why. If they are not performing to expectations, tell them what they are or are not doing that is getting in the way of meeting these expectations.

Share as much as you can—Provide links and resources that allow for more in-depth information or research.

Be consistent—Inconsistencies in talk or actions become even more visible in a transparent organization. Growing up playing video games taught Millennials how the rules form the game. When the rules shift at someone's whim, it does not make sense to Millennials and causes them to doubt and mistrust what you say.

Provide line-of-sight information—Provide as much information as possible to help Millennials understand what is not visible. The greater their line of sight and the more you connect the dots for them, the more connected and engaged their performance will be. Do your Millennials (or anyone else on your team, for that matter) understand how their work contributes to the company's performance?

Be a model of integrity—How well managers communicate and "walk the talk" goes miles with Millennials.

The Rubric Generation

In school, Millennials learned to live academically by the parameters of the rubric. When "rubric" is used in education, it refers to the methods of establishing assessment tools or rules for educators to use for scoring tests and giving grades. Using a set of criteria and standards of learning objectives to determine a student's performance on papers, projects, essays, and other assignments creates a rubric. Rubrics allow for standardized evaluation according to specified criteria, making grading simpler and more transparent. (See how that transparency concept keeps showing up!)

The rubric methodology is a way to define and create consistent assessment criteria. It allows both teachers and students to objectively assess complex or subjective assignments while providing grounds for self-evaluation, reflection, and peer review. The rubric provides a clear structure and measurement system so you can determine whether "A," "B," or "C" work is produced. These guidelines have been the way many Millennials were educated. They are accustomed to understanding how things will be judged and graded. As they arrive in the workplace, they are looking for the same direction and structure. They want to understand how to get an "A"!

As part of the boundary conversations you will be having, keep in mind that Millennials are looking for guidance on how things are judged, what the priorities are, and how they will be held accountable. Millennials need to understand what is expected of them on the job in terms of work output, timeframes, participation, and key deliverables.

A rubric workplace conversation should include the following questions:

- What is the job or task?

- Why does the job or task need to be done?

- How should the job or task be completed?

- When does the job or task need to be completed?

- What does an "A" job completion look like?

- If this task is determined to be acceptable at a pass/fail level, what does that look like?

⏱ *Millennial Minute*

As you stop trying to impose all the beliefs that accompany your generational mindset about how subordinates *should* behave, and instead begin to accept the wonderful gifts that Millennial employees bring, you will begin to reap the benefits from their contributions, innovations, and creativity.

●　　●　　●　　●　　●　　●　　●　　●　　●　　●　　●　　●　　●　　●　　●　　●　　●　　●

Creating the Rubric for Assessment

Define performance	"A" performance	"B" performance	"C" performance	"D" performance
Expectations				
Communication				
Boundaries				
Department Standards				
Punctuality/ Attendance				
Attire				
Workplace norms				

The chart above provides a framework to begin the process of developing a rubric for your Millennial employees or colleagues to help them understand what the varying levels of performance look and sound like in your world. An interesting paradox about the Millennials is their ability to do tasks that seem complex while they stumble over things that seem so basic. One Millennial, who works in a high-tech environment, had no idea how to fax a document. Imagine someone with a college degree, seemingly very smart, who has never had to fax anything!

To provide an example of how a large organization is working to better connect the multi-generations and provide an environment that is doing just that, here is an example. GenNext is an Employee Resource Group (ERG) at Southern California Edison that came together when Jacob Moore, a Millennial, and one of the group's founding members, wanted to encourage dialogue about the multi-generations' perspectives in the workplace as they attempt to positively influence the culture. The following article was written with support by Jacob Moore. I've had the opportunity to sit in on some of these meetings and observe the group as they continue to make connections and provide points of dialogue that unite, rather than divide, the multi-generations. Each of these meetings has a focus and purpose. The meetings are well attended and their participation has been very active. They also offer web access options, so even if you are not able to attend in person, you can attend virtually.

GenNext at Southern California Edison

A discussion provided by Jacob Moore, Program/Project Analyst, Southern California Edison

With half its workforce nearing retirement age, Southern California Edison (SCE) faced the potential loss of knowledge about its customers, marketplace, products and services, systems, processes, and culture. Chris Cabrera, communications project manager, and Jacob Moore, program/project analyst at SCE, detail how an employee resource group was developed to encourage knowledge transfer and promote technology for more effective collaboration across the organization.

We have four different generations in the workforce at SCE (Traditionalists, Baby Boomers, Gen X, and Gen Y), approximately 50 percent of which is made up of Baby Boomers. As Boomers near retirement age, Millennials will come to dominate the workforce. This presents a couple of challenges: not only do we have the task of replacing the labor force when our baby boomers retire, but we also have to maintain a competitive edge in the absence of their knowledge.

We looked at what steps the company could take to improve the SCE work environment, to retain and recruit Millennials, and how we could use the processes and tools that are so familiar to this generation to help the transfer of knowledge, while at the same time teaching the existing generation to use them.

The answer was GenNext—an employee resource group with a mission to strengthen the workforce by bridging generational gaps among our people. GenNext was developed from an existing "reverse mentoring" relationship between Lisa Cagnolatti, vice president of the business customer division of SCE's customer service business unit, and then-intern Jacob Moore. In their meetings, Moore would teach Cagnolatti about different technologies and how mediums such as Twitter and Facebook could be leveraged into the way we do business and communicate both externally and internally.

The key objectives of GenNext are to provide a meaningful forum to increase awareness of generational differences and to develop ideas to enable our multigenerational workforce to:

- Share knowledge across the company to drive mutual respect, teamwork, and innovation

- Embrace the value of all generations (especially the style of younger workers) to transform the SCE culture

- Promote technology and new tools to share best practices and connect information, resources, and people across the company

One of the main hurdles of a special interest group like GenNext is that it isn't our members' day job; everybody has their own full-time position at SCE. Getting involved and participating in groups is considered extra-curricular, so it's of key importance that we address the "What's in it for me?" question.

One event that always sells out is the Next Connection event. A networking opportunity, it uses the speed-dating concept and sees members lunch together with executives rotating tables every ten minutes to talk to a new group of employees. We also have a social media tool, Lotus Connections, where every employee has a profile on which they can post blog stories and form community groups. It's a place where we start discussions and post information and resources to get conversations going.

Outcome and the Future

After our events, we follow up with surveys and informal polls to find out what worked, what didn't, and how we can improve. In our informal feedback, our members have expressed that they love having the opportunity to get to know the executives—as it's something they wouldn't normally be able to do—and learn about new technology to better share knowledge and collaborate.

One big return on investment is our membership size, which has grown to four hundred, and our teams have increased as well. Our members are now willingly getting involved in event planning, leaving the board more time to spend on strategy and the direction of the group.

For the communication function, it has provided more exposure to senior leadership across the organization both as a team and one-on-one level to transform the SCE culture, to promote technology and new tools to share best practices and connect information, resources and people across the company. We set out to achieve these in three ways: by creating awareness, creating connections, and adopting new technology.

Spreading the Mission

When we first told people our mission, most didn't quite understand our purpose, so we ended up spending the first couple of years educating employees. In the first month, we published an article on our company intranet, The Portal, which promoted what GenNext was about, what we were going to do, and what we wanted to accomplish. We also added a rotating banner on some of our intranet pages to keep it front of mind.

We held a kick-off meeting, which introduced GenNext members to our project teams and provided the opportunity to discuss the role of each team member. We visited various departmental meetings, did road shows and "brown bag" lunches, and participated in outside fairs in the courtyard of the SCE headquarters, including safety and celebrations fairs where we would have a booth to answer any questions.

We also brought in generational experts to facilitate focus groups to educate the workforce on the challenges the company faces and the opportunities we have to work better together.

Key Takeaways for Achieving Insight
to Better Understand Gen Ys

They have Helicopter Parents (parents who fly low and hover!) who continue to parent and coach them.

♦ They expect their supervisors to take over where their devoted parents have left off.

They are the "Trophy Kids"—they are the pride and joy of their parents and often everybody gets an award for just being on the team, even if they have only played a few minutes during an entire season!

They are not comfortable with conflict and have not had much experience with conflict resolution because their parents smoothed the road for them in order to keep things calm.

They are accustomed to structured lives because they have had scheduled daily plans since they were young.

They want to know *why*—they've been encouraged to ask questions.

They want lots of **feedback** and coaching.

They want **transparency** and to be able to trust others.

They know how to quickly obtain data and will use their strong social network to find what they are after.

They want **flexibility** in all aspects of their work.

They are good collaborators and know how to work on a team.

They are **risk adverse** because they do not have experience failing and are worried that they won't know how to navigate a situation in which they are not successful.

They have tattoos and piercings and see these as part of their identification with their generation, as a visible display of their brand.

They don't perceive themselves as entitled. They just expect what they expect.

✦ 2 ✦

Understanding Gen Ys
POTENTIAL

*POTENTIAL: having or showing the capacity to become
or develop into something in the future.*

Members of Generation Y have been raised to believe they can do anything they want, even when others perceive that their ideas are a bit "out there"! With social networking, blogging, and the popularity of being discovered on shows like American Idol, becoming famous no longer seems impossible. As a result, Millennials see their world as being full of potential.

As tech-savvy digital natives, Millennials have grown up with the Internet, connectivity, instant communication, and the ability to obtain information quickly. This has impacted the generation in many ways. Their parents relied on them to help with the household technology—whether that was figuring out how to use the DVR, transfer photos from a digital camera to a computer, or import their CD library to their computer—so they became the resident experts, the "go-to persons" to help manage the family's technology. This knowledge equated power, reaching a sort of equality with their parents, becoming collaborators, not just dependent offspring.

This generation's mostly baby boomer parents see their children as an extension of themselves and have invested a lot of time, emotion, and energy in them. Many baby boomer moms had become corporate leaders, managers, and entrepreneurs, accruing the many skills that business leadership develops. In the spirit of "performance improvement," these moms applied the same developmental and coaching skills to their children that they utilized with their staffs. An interesting fact about these 75 million young people is that "only children" make up 25 percent of their number. Consequently, they were not asked to share their parents' time with siblings. In short, Millennials became accustomed to being heard and having their opinions matter.

As these Millennials come to the workplace, their expectations are very different from those of the generations before them. One of the challenges is that we are asking this generation to assimilate into a company in the same way the previous generations did. There is not enough thought about how they best learn and work, or how to maximize their tech skills to use their great potential to make contributions to your department, team, or business. POTENTIAL works both ways. This chapter challenges you to look at how and why they perceive themselves as they do, why their tattoos and the stereotype of the label of "entitlement" surrounds them, and how to utilize a new perspective in order to leverage their amazing POTENTIAL. What's in it for you? The more you tap into the POTENTIAL of those around you, the greater their contribution, and the easier your job will become.

⏰ MILLENNIAL MINUTE

Unbundle your thoughts about entitlement by sorting out the areas in which your Millennials appear to feel "entitled." These could include expectation about being promoted quickly, scheduling, selection of work, choice of teammates, or choices about how the work is to be completed. Then, have a conversation about those specific areas so you can obtain clarity from their point of view and share your perspective and clarify expectations.

* * * * * * * * * * * * * * * * * * *

What's with the Tattoos?

There has been a resurgence of tattoos in many parts of the world and they have gained enormous popularity with Millennials. The growth in tattoo culture has produced many new artists in the industry, many of whom have technical or fine arts training. Coupled with advancements in tattoo pigments and the ongoing refinement of tattoo equipment, the quality of tattoos being created has greatly improved.

A tattoo or dermal pigmentation is a mark made by inserting pigment into the skin for decorative or other reasons. The word "tattoo" comes from the Tahitian "tatu" which means "to mark something."

Tattooing is a worldwide practice. The Ainu, the indigenous people of Japan, wore facial tattoos. Tattooing was widespread among Polynesian peoples and among certain tribal groups in the Philippines, Borneo, Mentawai, Africa, North America, South America, Europe, Cambodia, and China. Despite some taboos surrounding tattooing, the art continues to be popular all over the world.

Dave Navarro, an American guitarist, provides this perspective: "My skin is my canvas. The artwork on it represents something that is very powerful and meaningful in my life. I look at my skin as something of a living diary because all my tattoos represent a time in my life. And I never wish to shut the door on the past, so I carry it all with me."

So many Millennials see tattoos as a part of their brand, reflecting to the world who they are, what has meaning to them, and their life's purpose. Tattoos can be a reflection into the Millennial's soul. Tattoos often serve as a way to share what they perceive to be important, and reflect many elements that can provide insight into their belief system. Asking about their tattoo(s) is a great way to find out more about this person.

Regardless of your own beliefs about tattoos, imagine it as a painting, maybe not your personal style of artistry, but a painting that the artist created to tell a story, to share a perspective and illustrate their brand.

⏱ MILLENNIAL MINUTE

Among Americans, 32 percent[7] of those between the ages of twenty-five and twenty-nine have a tattoo, compared to 25 percent of those in their thirties and 12 percent of those in their forties. Tattoos are called tats and those creating these tats are called artists.

● ● ● ● ● ● ● ● ● ● ● ● ● ● ● ● ● ●

How to Engage in a Conversation about Tattoos

Here are some questions to help you connect and begin a conversation. Start by focusing on one of the visible tattoos.

"Tell me about the tattoo on your ankle."

"Tell me about the artist."

"What's unique or special about this artist?"

"Which tattoo is your favorite? Why is it your favorite?"

"How do these tattoos tell the world who you are?"

"If you could add another tattoo tomorrow, and time and money were not an issue, what would you select?"

"Hypothetically, if you were offered a substantial promotion and pay raise, but had to keep your tattoos covered, would you accept these terms? Why or why not?"

✳ *Case Study*

The following case study is an example of how asking about a tattoo can open the door to further understanding. As such, when you ask about their tattoos, what they mean, and why they have them, you will learn much more than you might have imagined, which will support your ability to see their potential in a new light.

Betty is a seasoned manager working in the traditional environment of an insurance company where she has been employed for over twenty years. Betty is a calm leader and a good mentor. One of the things Betty does not understand is the rampant spread of tattoos appearing on the younger generation. Why do they want to mark up their bodies? Do they not realize that as they age, twenty years from now, these tattoos will no longer be in the same place?

Betty's newest employee is a young man named Luke who has been working for the company for two years, but recently transferred into Betty's department. Betty likes that Luke seems to keep to himself. She has no tolerance for hearing about the details of these Millennials' lives, which seem so self-indulgent. (Have you seen what they post on Facebook? Do I really care what YOU had for lunch or that you're in a bad mood?)

As the office air-conditioning has not been working properly, everyone has rolled up their sleeves and Betty realizes that Luke has tattoos on his upper arms. The tattoos are colorful and look intense. Betty grabs the opportunity to ask Luke about them (did she really want to know??) because she knows so little about him and he's not very talkative.

Betty: *Luke, your tattoos are so colorful and look interesting, tell me what the one on your right arm means.*

Luke: (In a quiet voice) *This one is actually very personal. It represents my faith and my devotion. I have my grandfather's name on this arm* *because he was the reason I became so interested in religion. He was my best friend while I was growing up, and in so many ways I had a lot more in common with him than I did with my parents. When he became ill a few years ago and knew his days were numbered, we worked together to figure out a fitting tattoo, style, and color and to find the right artist. I don't know if you are familiar with the whole tattoo scene, but the people who do the work view themselves as artists.*

Betty: *No, I'm not familiar with tattooing and I had no idea how detailed and meaningful tattoos could be. Has this artist done other tattoos for you?*

Luke: *(His voice and conviction getting stronger) Yes, I have tattoos on the tops of both of my feet. One is a soccer ball, a tribute to my favorite sport; I love the game and played all through college and still play on the weekends. On the other foot I have "NCC-1701" and a picture of the Starship Enterprise because I'm a devoted trekkie.*

Betty: *I understand the soccer ball, but what do you like so much about* Star Trek?

Luke: *To me,* Star Trek *was a show about hope. Roddenberry had a vision, and that vision came across every week in the configuration of the show: a multiethnic, integrated planet Earth exploring the galaxy. On an intellectual level, the show appealed as most science fiction does, with speculative science that was engaging. Transporters, phasers, warp drive. It's all pretty cool stuff, and real in theory, given the discussions being held by cosmologists and physicists at the time. And of course, wrapping this all together in the best instances was character-driven story telling. The stories still work, like Shakespeare does hundreds of years later, because people connect with the characters. They are ordinary people reacting to extraordinary circumstances.*

Betty: *Thank you so much for sharing all of that! Your insights are thought-provoking, and I look forward to continued conversations.*

So What Transpired Here?

In a very short time, and with some good questions, Betty opened a communication channel with Luke and discovered a lot of new things about his interests and the way he thinks. Luke is sentimental, and if he had such a wonderful relationship with his grandfather, he is most likely also able to connect with more mature colleagues. He's athletic and continues to play soccer, and he succinctly articulated the intellectual aspects of Star Trek. Betty is realizing how much more Luke has going on than she realized and she needs to continue to find ways to reach into his potential so he will become even more engaged and effective.

Let them tell you *their* story. The purpose of asking these questions is to learn more about the person behind the tattoos. Opening the conversation up will allow you to tap into a world of potential. This will then lead to other conversations. You will be pleasantly surprised by what you learn and how this simple act of questioning and listening can yield insight and lay the foundation for a solid business relationship.

🕐 Millennial Minute

As a way to honor their father who had passed away from cancer, a young adult family of siblings had their fathers' signature tattooed on their arms to honor his memory and keep him "close" in their thoughts.

• • • • • • • • • • • • • • • • • • •

Why So Entitled?

Entitlement is a word that has often been applied to the Millennials. Entitlement is typically applied to those who think they have the right to something, whether it is a job, a promotion, or inclusion in key decisions. Why does this generation appear entitled?

Because many Baby Boomer and Generation X parents:

- did not let their children fail
- never let their children think they were "losers," only winners, whether or not the game or activity score indicated otherwise
- let their children know they were special for just being "them"
- did not demand they get summer jobs, instead making sure they went on great trips, to exciting camps, and had experiences that would increase their chances of getting into a great college

EVERYTHING they did was applauded. They were given constant praise, feedback, and kudos. "No" was not a big part of the parenting style. If their team did not bring home the trophy, often their parents bought them one. If they did not get a good grade in school or on a paper, their parents called the teacher. Boomer parents made things happen. Boomer moms had been in the workplace and were happy to manage whatever needed to be done to make this generation feel good about themselves. Self-esteem was the guide, and anything deemed to harm that sense of self was dismissed, moved aside, or changed in course.

Gen Ys do not work well with harsh bosses and will walk away from a job if diplomacy and coaching are not part of the work environment. Though their baby boomer parents were always happy to have a job, this being one of their core values, Gen Y's perception is that they have options. As 50 percent of them live with one or both of their parents into their mid-twenties and they typically have favorable relationships, this provides choices. Changing jobs several times in a year, means resume and skill building. According to Mark McCrindle, a social researcher, it's currently estimated that each Gen Y will have five careers and twenty employers across their working lifetime. Applying what they have learned and experienced is the mindset. Being the last hired into a company also means the possibility of being the first to be let go when the economy is bad, as has been the case for many Gen Ys, so they are prepared to consistently update their resumes. Being labeled as a "job-hopper" is not part of this generation's vocabulary and is an idea that seems archaic.

🕐 **MILLENNIAL MINUTE**

Millennials are looking for self-fulfillment—not just work.

● ● ● ● ● ● ● ● ● ● ● ● ● ● ● ● ● ● ●

How to Talk to Someone Who Appears Entitled

Here are some questions to help you go beyond the "entitlement" mindset and get to the root of a Millennial's perspective.

What skills do you possess that lead you to believe you are ready for this promotion?

The idea is to lead them down the path of a logical decision—

what skills do you possess that make you right for this assignment/position? This takes the emotion out and allows for an adult conversation.

I know you think you are ready for a promotion, so let's review the skill requirements for this position and discuss what it takes to successfully manage it.

This question frames their skills against the skills and attributes needed and asks them to rationally explain why they believe they are ready. As you continue to ask specific questions about specific skills, they will realize they are not yet ready for the position. Because they were able to reach this conclusion on their own, they will feel comfortable that this is a business decision, not a personal one.

The reason I need you to do it this way is that it makes sense for the customer.

Understanding the reason *why* something needs to be done a certain way is key to helping someone who appears entitled to buy into an idea. Millennials are smart and want to do the right thing, but for it to make sense, they need to know why.

What are the top three things that you like to have in your work environment to feel motivated?

It may include asking you for ongoing feedback, asking to have input on a project's direction, or being included in all aspects of a project. The most important thing is to *ask* them; they will be happy to share.

What challenges and opportunities do you believe you are ready for next?

This will help you understand what they are thinking and how that aligns with your perspectives. Understanding their frame of mind allows you to ask clarifying questions and be able to conduct a meaningful conversation.

Declare your intentions by letting the Millennial know *why* you are asking questions or providing information. "I am interested in your achievements because I see a lot of potential. You bring a lot to this job, and I want to be sure you have what you need to be successful."

⏱ *MILLENNIAL MINUTE*

Millennials are motivated by transparency—they want to see as much as they can and want you, as their supervisor, to be honest and straightforward. With their vast social networks (the average Millennial has more than 250 friends on Facebook), checking on information and verifying data is fast and easy—they will keep checking, even if you do not choose to provide the requested information.

• • • • • • • • • • • • • • • • • • • •

Partner Mentoring

As ongoing learning is a part of the Millennial mindset, connecting them with a mentor is a great way to impart information as you demonstrate your commitment to their development. Having someone work with and coach them individually appeals to their need to learn more in a way that allows them to have a say in *what* they are learning, *who* is providing the information, and *what* they will learn or gain from this time.

One element that is different from the traditional mentoring concept is that Gen Ys need to be a part of the process by reciprocating through contributions related to their areas of expertise. This comes from their being asked as they were growing up how things worked, especially electronic things. Through this they came to believe that they were partners, not just kids. Because Gen Ys see mentoring as bidirectional, it is important that they see others recognizing their value. If the organization values the knowledge and experience they bring with them, even if that experience comes from gaming or social media, they'll want to contribute their skills. You'll be enriching the experience of those they partner with as well as enhancing the work ambiance and creating stronger working relationships.

Speaking of work ambience, that typical greeting of "hey dude" applies consistently to everyone in their social world, and those more accustomed to the traditional rank and file military protocol are always surprised when they hear this greeting!

Since their generation is tech-savvy, they know how to obtain information quickly, how to communicate fast, and how to leverage their social networks. They are ideal teachers because they can be subject-matter experts in many areas. Tap into this great natural resource by having your Millennial mentor someone on the team, even someone on the team from a different generation. This sets up a win-win framework. It sends a message that everyone has something to share or teach and that the old-fashioned management hierarchy that says you must be a manager or director to be a mentor should not bind you. This way of partner-mentoring is especially important in the onboarding process as you bring Gen Y talent into your company or department. Millennials do not want to just be the recipient of information, they want to ask questions, contribute, and be able to make their mark—even on the first day of employment. Today's younger workers have things to teach the company, and if the firm doesn't reciprocate early on by acknowledging that, then the onboarding process may be very close to the exit interview.

⏱ MILLENNIAL MINUTE

Lunch & Learn—Invite Millennials to share knowledge and skills they have about social networking, computer tricks and shortcuts, or an area in which they have expertise. Invite coworkers, especially those from different departments or generations, and ask them to share their areas of expertise, skills, and knowledge. Potential is leveraged by tapping into everyone's strengths.

• • • • • • • • • • • • • • • • • •

What Motivates Millennials?

Though work–life balance was initially a Gen X goal, Generation Y sees this as a "must have" and it's the cornerstone of what motivates them. Interestingly, Baby Boomers are also looking to have more balance in their work life as many are still supporting kids in addition to aging parents. Work–life balance puts the focus on work in a new light. Gen Ys don't typically define a "good job" by how much it pays but by how well it fits into their lives, the quality of the work, and the tone of the environment.

Millennial motivation is different than that of any previous generation; they are less focused on a big salary, although they want to be paid well, preferring perks like tuition reimbursement, flexible spending accounts, and even pet insurance when offered, as well as the ability to telecommute. Job satisfaction and feeling engaged is more important than a large paycheck, and the factors that they use to identify a good job can include consistent coaching, a friendly work environment, and promotional or learning opportunities.

However, these very socially networked and connected younger workers are the first to raise their hands if they perceive that they are being treated inappropriately or unfairly. They will question established rules and processes and ask tough questions without concern for appearing politically savvy. Loyalty and job satisfaction can be encouraged when you involve them in decision-making and respect their opinions by listening.

Those on your team or those who you work with will be more than happy to share what motivates them, just ask! As students, teachers made them aware of their learning style and how they best acquire information. The more connected and informed they feel, the more motivated they will be to do a good job. Remember, they always want to know why, so share as much as you can and keep the dialogue open and honest.

⏰ MILLENNIAL MINUTE

Millennials grew up in the age of the Internet and are often referred to as "digital natives." They are accustomed to being barraged with immense amounts of information and data at all times and have a natural ability to gather information from diverse sources. With regard to technology, their frame of reference is much different from previous generations for whom technological advances came with vast improvements in the quality of life. Millennials inherited an automated, technologically advanced existence and this is what they know. They don't remember a time without computers, cell phones, ATMs, the Internet, or social media. They tend to be early adopters of new technology products and services, as they have no fear of "pressing the wrong button," which some of their parents would admit to!

Do You Need a Generational Resource Group?*

The following includes excerpts from Diversity Inc. magazine and highlights a variety of companies that are utilizing Generational Resource Groups with a great deal of success.

Gideon Hyacinth, age 28, joined Dell, listed number 30 in The 2011 DiversityInc Top 50 Companies for Diversity, two and a half years ago. He noticed quickly that there were a lot of young people, right out of college, working in their cubicles pretty much in isolation. (GRC)

"There was no way for us to connect with each other. We didn't know how to network or have an impact on the company," recalls Hyacinth, an HR business generalist.

With two of his twentysomething peers, Hyacinth formed GenNext, an employee-resource group. The goal was professional and leadership development, an increased sense of community and the ability to help the company reach younger consumers. They started in November 2009 with twenty people in the room. They now have more than seven hundred members in three countries—the United States, Panama, and India—and are launching a chapter in Brazil.

The group is proving itself invaluable, says Michael Tatelman, age 54, vice president and general manager of North American Consumer Sales and the group's executive sponsor. For example, when Dell was developing Streak, its mobile tablet, it consulted with group members about what features and applications would most appeal to younger users.

Two companies that have strong generational outreach but have chosen not to have formal generational ERGs are Deloitte, which has pioneered generational research, and Cox, which creates diversity councils that span various demographics, including age.

Suzanne Skipper, a principal in Deloitte Consulting, says Deloitte decided against creating distinct ERGs but instead chose to "bake into all of our ERGs those sorts of activities that the Gen Y-ers are going to identify with. For us, it was about integrating and creating meaningful, purposeful organizations and structures, like blogs and social networking, to drive engagement."

Mae Douglas, executive vice president and chief people officer at Cox, says age is integrated in all of their nine local diversity councils, but Cox chooses not to have groups specifically identified by one demographic. "We get a quarterly report and we measure their age diversity," she notes.

WellPoint's younger-employees group, HYPE (Healthcare Young Professionals Exchange), has been helpful in finding out ways to enable Millennials to stick around longer, notes Linda Jimenez, chief diversity officer and staff vice president, diversity and inclusion. "It is about asking very particularly what it is they want, individually . . . If you recognize that they are not here for ten years, what opportunities exist within our organization?" she asks.

She notes that for Millennials, having an impact on the community is a key factor in engagement and retention.

"What really attracts this age group? That commitment to making a difference. That social responsibility, that volunteerism, is a really attractive component for them," Jimenez says.

Aetna is one of the biggest success stories. In addition to EnRGy, Aetna started the X Factor ERG in the fourth quarter of 2009 and the BoomER Group in January 2009. Today, X Factor has 833 members and BoomER Group has 639 members. [8]

Key Takeaways for Engaging Millennials to Achieve Their Full Potential

✦ Entitlement for them is basically what we call their feeling of having privileges. It should be understood what "entitlement" means to a Millennial—it's just what they know from their upbringing and are familiar with. Being asked their opinions and having a voice in all things that connect to their lives is how they have been raised and socialized. Because fostering positive self-esteem was their parents' guide and mantra, they are familiar with being rewarded for just *being* on the team, whether or not they played, being applauded for making the effort, even when those efforts did not lead to success. Gen Ys do not work well with harsh bosses, and if diplomacy and coaching are not a part of the work environment, they will not perform effectively and may even walk away from the job. Try refocusing your perspective and think of it not as entitlement, but as potential. Imagine what could happen to effectiveness when you mine and cultivate Millennials' talents and skills and engage their focused concentration on the work at hand, tapping into all of the great things they can bring to the job.

✦ Feedback and coaching have been constants for Millennials. As you continue to provide coaching and constructive feedback, they will quickly respond to that information and apply it to their jobs and tasks. IF you utilize the mindset that "when I was their age I didn't need so much feedback," you are compromising your ability to engage this smart and motivated generation, which is doing exactly what it's been taught to do—respond to coaching, apply feedback to enhance performance, move forward, and request additional coaching and feedback.

✦ Boundaries have a different meaning to Millennials than they may to you and others on your team. As the first global generation, they have not known a world without Internet access, they are connected 24/7. Millennials appear in the workplace without a boundaries frame of mind. They believe, as they have been told, that they are bright, educated, and important and that they have much to contribute starting right now. They feel just fine questioning a CEO or any executive, coming to work in casual clothing, and texting and talking on their phone as it suits them. Engage them by setting clear expectations for your environment's boundaries. It may seem like "common sense" to you, but providing clear expectations about dress, office demeanor, cell phone use, the nuances of your business, and the general boundaries required by your specific environment will save you a lot of time and anxiety down the road. Utilize the phrase "You don't know what you don't know" to help you understand that, although this generation is very smart, some of the things that may seem like common sense to you are completely alien to them!

✦ Transparency has changed the way business is conducted and impacted the expectation of all employees, especially Millennials. Transparency matters in business because your customers, as well as your employees, know a lot about you and your business and there is far greater access to this information and speed at which it can be shared. Be as honest as you can about what's occurring in your business. Their ability to connect with the many social networks they belong to can provide them with information on many levels—it's just a few clicks away.

♦ Rubric-generation thinking—Millennials understand this scoring tool and respond favorably when they know not just what's expected of them, but what it takes to excel at a particular assignment and what it takes to meet acceptable standards. The rubric is an attempt to define consistent assessment criteria and set a clear performance expectation for what is required, including when and how it is to be delivered. Use this to engage your Millennials—they will respond favorably to having this level of clarity. Millennials can be dedicated workers once they are clear on direction and are helped to see "what's in it for them." From your perspective, providing the benefits of what they will learn may seem like coddling or indulging them, but these few minutes will help their skill set and, in turn, actually help you, as they respond favorably to understanding the parameters of the assignment.

♦ Consistency in actions and words is something that Millennials pay close attention to as they observe the people in their work environment. For example, if a Millennial on your team was called out for wearing an outfit that was too suggestive, such as a low-cut tank top, skimpy shirt, or too-short skirt, but one of the female executives was seen wearing basically the same outfit without reprimand, it's unlikely that this inconsistency would be overlooked. Now, you could make the argument that it's not just Millennials who notice inconsistencies; people of other generations also notice when things do not align. But Millennials' perception is that hierarchal boundaries do not exist in the same way that previous generations believe they do. As a result, they believe that it's okay to challenge, push back, and let their bosses know how they really feel. Unlike the generations before them, Millennials also have the power of their social network and the ability to instantly communicate their disgust—and they do not hesitate to do so!

✦ 3 ✦

What TRUST means to Gen Ys

TRUST: confidence in and reliance on good qualities
especially fairness, truth, honor, and ability.

What is trust? While the common definition of trust is based on believing in the possibility of relying on the good qualities of others, the meaning takes many different forms in a work environment. There is the trust that an employee has in the company, in the team, and in you, the boss. Much of the world is wary about institutions and businesses that have violated our trust. *Harvard Business Review's* June 2009 issue titled "Rebuilding Trust" was devoted to this concept. Trust is a fluid entity which continually changes.

Trust in humans also has a physiological base. When high levels of oxytocin are present in the brain, people are more apt to trust. High oxytocin levels also reduce fear. Though "to trust or not to trust" is not wholly dependent on brain chemicals, there is a chemistry of trust.[9]

Millennials do not trust easily and with sound reasons. They have known many unfortunate events that shaped their perception of trust and truth, including a presidential impeachment, Desert Storm, the Oklahoma City bombing, the Columbine High School shootings, September 11, the implosion of Enron, WorldCom, and peoples' losses during the Great Recession. Their experiences have told them to be cautious and sometimes skeptical, especially when corporations are involved.

Much has been written about corporate loyalty. Mercer,[10] the giant New York City-based human resources consulting firm, surveyed 30,000 employees in 17 spots around the globe between the fourth quarter of 2010 and the second quarter of 2011. Not surprisingly, the number of workers who are seriously considering moving on from their jobs has increased since the last time Mercer did the survey, between 2003 and 2006, before the Great Recession. In the United States the percentage of workers who said they wanted to leave and get a new job rose nine percentage points, from 23 percent in 2005 to about one in three, or 32 percent, in 2010. And there can be no loyalty to a corporation without trust. As Millennials watched their parents become victims of the no-rewards, fifty-hour-plus workweek, they clearly received the message that there is no benefit to remaining loyal to an employer. Can you blame them? Millennials have experienced that nothing is permanent —everything is fluid.

Low trust causes friction. Low trust creates hidden agendas, politics, interpersonal conflict, win–lose thinking, and defensive and self-protective communication among people. Low trust slows everything down—decisions, communication, and relationships.

High turnover reduces trust. When your workforce is exiting, it becomes the "rats on the sinking ship" syndrome. People get nervous and worry that those people leaving know something they do not.

What Does Trust Mean in the Workplace?

Trust is a currency that Millennials value highly. Once trust is broken, the currency's value drops significantly. Ask your Millennials what trust in the workplace means to them, especially as it relates to their relationship with their supervisor. Do the Millennials on your team trust you?

Millennials have the freedom to test boundaries in a way no generation before them had, and they do so daily. In a recent Randstad survey,[11] among the top traits for an ideal employer to have was "providing a workplace that reflects its respect for me and my coworkers." As one college senior put it, "As a manager, understanding our desire to be heard and acknowledged can help the company's future."

Millennials know they're new to the workplace, but they want leadership and good role models and to know that their ideals are valued and important to the team. They've been team players since elementary school and, through their upbringing, were always taught that their ideas were as important as anyone else's, regardless of age or skill set. They expect the same in the workplace.

When supervisors hold staff meetings and don't let others speak, and specifically don't listen to what the newer employees are thinking and feeling, these newer people tend to feel isolated and are less likely to want to participate in the future, becoming less apt to trust their managers. They begin tuning out and complaining rather than engaging, listening, and learning, and the seeds of doubt are planted. Productivity definitely goes down when they feel separated from the team and are not respected.

Gen Ys want to see that their ideas are treated respectfully, even though they have not been around that long.

Improving Trust by Investing Trust

In order to engage and lead, creating a relationship of trust and ultimately an environment of trust allows you to move the obstacles that are created when there is low trust or no trust within your team, especially for those Millennials who have been raised to be skeptical. TRUST is workplace currency for them.

Because trust is the currency for Millennials, fully investing yourself will pay dividends to these business relationships. Accumulate trust by trying the following:

1. *Deliver daily on your commitments.*

   When you say you are going to do something, do it!

2. *Visibly and verbally respect all others.*

   When speaking ill of another, the Millennial listening to this assumes you will be talking in the same negative way about them when they are not present.

3. *Be as transparent as possible.*

   Be as honest and transparent as you professionally are able; Millennials respond well to truth, even if it is not something they want to hear.

4. *Encourage people to learn from mistakes.*

   Create an environment where mistakes are okay as long as you learn from them and don't repeat them.

5. *Refrain from "generation bashing" or stereotyping others.*

   Millennials are sensitive to generalizations, whether about themselves or other generations.

6. *Trust begets trust.*

The more you demonstrate to others that you trust them and that your actions and words are consistent with trust behaviors, the more others will trust you.

7. *Provide a "heads-up," not a "gotcha."*

Give your Millennial a heads-up to help them in appropriate situations. For example, let them know when they should be dressing more nicely for a meeting or when customers or clients will be in the office. Asking them to "step it up" and sharing why it is important will contribute to the trust factor. Catching them after the fact (gotcha!) does nothing to promote trust and shows them that you are not really interested in their success.

The Results-Only Work Environment

A revolutionary strategy called Results-Only Work Environment (ROWE) has created the ultimate situation for workplace trust. This paradigm shifting strategy created by the consulting company CultureRx provides a new model that allows employees to be paid and rewarded only for the results of their work. The goal is to keep workers who deliver good results engaged and motivated. Jody Thompson and Cali Ressler's book, *Why Work Sucks and How to Fix It: No Schedules, No Meetings, No Joke—The Simple Change That Can Make Your Job Terrific*[12] chronicles the ROWE programs they have done at Best Buy and other companies.

In a ROWE workplace the authors describe an environment where it is the performance that counts, not the number of hours worked, or the way time is spent on the job. They explain:

- Why there is no need for schedules
- Why nobody focuses on "How many hours did you work?"
- Why nobody feels overworked, stressed out, or guilty
- Why "work" is not a place where you go; it's something you do
- Why people at all levels stop wasting the company's time and money
- Why teamwork, morale, and engagement soar
- Why there's no judgment made on how people spend their time

The foundation of this strategy is trust. Trust that you will do the work even when not directly supervised. There is a myth in business that if I can't SEE you working, you aren't! Well, you could look very busy and be reading articles, even shopping online, and the boss does not always know the difference.

ROWE is all about results. No results, no job. It's that simple.

Trust Talk

The interesting thing about "trust talk" is that there are things you can say that will help to promote trust, but in the long run trust is really about what you do and how you behave. (And here we are back at transparency!) Millennials are very perceptive of the consistency of what you do and what you say. Here are some phrases to help you as you engage in conversations to promote trust, transparency, and honesty:

I don't know the answer but I'll find out and let you know.

Millennials do not discount your leadership skills if you don't know the answer, but they will "take points away" if you lie. Follow up with the answer and they are more apt to follow you!

I trust your good business judgment, so make the decision and let me know the outcome.

Empowering Millennials to make good decisions is essential to their becoming independent. Most likely they will ask for your guidance. Have them come back to you with their decision and role-play with them as if you were the client/customer and they were delivering the message. This allows you to check their thought process.

Though it was not easy, I'm glad you pointed out your concerns.

I'm confident in our ability to overcome this issue and we'll have a stronger relationship for having done so. Acknowledging that they are adults and you value their input goes a long way in working with a "we agree to disagree" process. Additionally, knowing how to discuss different perspectives in a respectful way will result in better decisions, better products, and great customer service.

I always appreciate your point of view, even though we may not always agree.

Letting your Millennial share their perspective is what they are accustomed to and what they want to do to create value.

Help me understand how you reached that decision.

When you ask your Millennial to explain their rationale, you are modeling good business thinking and making decisions based on reason and logic.

I wonder if we have the same information. My information leads me to a different conclusion.

Rather than "what the #@*! were you thinking," ask your Millennial to review their data, perhaps you aren't both working from the same page.

"Do they trust you?" seems to be a simple yes or no question. But it's actually a very deep and complex thought, as trust is viewed on so many levels. In a supervisory leadership role your employees, Gen Y and all others, are always judging. They will make judgments about trust based on these behaviors:

➤ Whether or not you are true to your word

➤ Whether you admit when you've provided incorrect information

➤ Whether you promise something and follow up appropriately

➤ Whether you admit the times when you don't know the answer

➤ Whether you talk negatively about others

Command and Control versus Collaboration

Millennials don't like to be micromanaged (does any adult?) and their tolerance for this in the workplace is low. But let's not forget that the need for CLARITY in regard to what is expected project-by-project is high. The need for clear direction is also high, along with what the desired outcomes and timelines are.

Millennials are inclusive because of the way they have been raised. Everyone on the team contributes, regardless of where they are from, their ethnicity or orientation. Being bombarded with data and content, they are challenged to know what is important, what info they can trust and count on. So, they count on their networks to sort it out and help with problem solving. When they can't make sense of it or determine its validity, they send it out to their networks and have faith in those they trust. Collaboration was a part of the American academic curriculum. Team teaching, team learning, the integration of topics—this was the framework in which many Millennials were educated. Command and control, an important style during a disaster, is not what will take you and your team to increased productivity in the long run. Look at the collaboration tools available: wikis, Google Docs, searchable discussion forums, and of course MySpace, Facebook, and other social networking sites.

The Rules of the Game: How a Generation of Digital Game Playing Affects Trust

Over 80 percent[13] of Millennials, and Gen Xers for that matter, play digital games, from Solitaire to Warhammer Online. The rules of these games are static: the challenges are defined, the rewards are established. In the rules of a game there are no office politics or other systems in which not everyone plays by the same rules or with the same resources. Millennials are well-equipped for turning to resources outside the system if that will help them conquer a challenge. What they are not as well equipped for is inconsistency. Consistency is critical in building trust with Millennials. Inconsistency in the workplace is certainly not a new concept, but what is different is that Millennials are not afraid to call out these inconsistencies, even when they involve those with a higher standing in the company.

The Impact of Conflict on Millennials

Conflict occurs for a variety of reasons, regardless of generational differences. Positive conflict, where relationships are strong and built on trust and respect, is not only healthy but desirable. Having different perspectives, opinions, ideas, and approaches makes for better processes, products, and innovation.

Negative conflict in the workplace can erode trust, undermine relationships, and impact effectiveness. Who hasn't been so angry with someone we worked with (or for!) that we were only too happy to sit and contemplate the many ways we could derail or disgrace them or dreamt (admit it!) of inflicting serious harm!

At the root of conflict is often a lack of clarity concerning intentions. Intentions allow us to understand what the other person is thinking, what is on their mind, or what they are planning. Sharing your clear intentions takes the guesswork out of a Millennial's mind. Let your team know your intentions—the more you share, the stronger the communication. The old adage that if you did not hear from your boss, everything was okay is not an effective management concept with Millennials. They want to feel connected and to know where you are coming from.

An example of setting an intention would be to let your Gen Y employee know *why* you are assigning a project or asking them to do something that might not be in their day-to-day stream of work. By letting the employee know that the reason you are asking for daily updates on a particular project is because of the sensitive nature of the topic or because it is of particular interest to your boss's boss, you are assuring them of your belief in their ability to adequately complete the job. When they do not *know* this aspect, they assume that the reason you are hovering is because you believe they are not capable, effective, or properly skilled.

Resolving Conflict

The following acronym will support you as you coach your Millennials to resolve conflict. The goal is to have your team figure out how to problem-solve with just a bit of feedback, so that eventually they will be able to work more independently. Here's some **H.E.L.P.**

Hear what they are upset about. Is it about you or do they just need to vent?

Encourage them to figure out the essence of the conflict. Is there a miscommunication? Misunderstanding? Disappointment?

Lead by example. When they see you remaining calm, with your voice and emotions under control, you provide a model of ways to brainstorm, and you lead by example.

Praise them as they manage problems and resolve conflicts.

✳ *Case Study*

Steve is a Baby Boomer and views himself as a young-at-heart boss! He appreciates the new qualities that Millennials are bringing to the workplace and, although they may require a different style of leadership from what he is accustomed to, he is willing to coach and mentor them in a style they appreciate and respond to because of the greater results.

Steve: *Hi Katie. You wanted to talk about an issue you were having?*

Katie: *Yes, I'm very upset. My team, they just don't like me! Since last week when I blew up, things have become so tense. I know I'm opinionated, but I thought the team was totally going in the wrong direction and I told them so. I can't work in this type of environment.*

Steve: *Okay, so let's take a step back and look at what happened. Being as objective as you can be, what did you say to the team that seemed to cause this tension?*

Katie: *Well, we were working on the new project and I know a lot about this. As we were working on what our ideas were to get started, the group began to go off on a tangent and was not letting me talk. I finally got so mad, I kinda' raised my voice and that really made them mad. After the meeting was over, I sent emails to everyone trying to explain my ideas again and not one of them returned the email and no one said good-bye to me when they left the office. It's been two days and no one is really talking to me, except if they absolutely have to.*

Steve: *You are obviously upset, but again being as objective as possible, after having thought about what occurred, what could you have done differently that might have changed the outcome?*

Katie: *I think many people on the team are jealous of me and they try to knock me down by being mean.*

Steve: *Katie, you have had a lot of wonderful experiences in your life and when you have had the opportunity to travel as much as you have, it affords a perspective that is wonderful, but do you really think they are jealous?*

Katie: *I don't mean to be conceited, but yes.*

Steve: *Let's assume they are jealous of you. Let's go back to the meeting and look at your behavior. What did you do in this meeting to be an effective team player? How well did you listen to others when they* *spoke? How often did you assume you knew what someone was going to say, so you tuned them out or jumped to conclusions? Did you really HEAR what they were offering or did you assume?*

Katie: *Well ... well, I just know that I'm right and they are not listening to me.*

Steve: *If I did not know you and I was listening to this conversation, I believe as an observer I would have the impression that you are arrogant and believe you know much more than others. How do you like working with people you think are arrogant?*

Katie: *Well, I don't like working with arrogant people. I had one that I had to deal with while I was interning and I think he was an idiot! But, (voice becoming quieter, more reflective) I guess I see what you mean if someone was listening to this conversation how they might think I was a little arrogant, which could have created the conflict.*

Steve: *What are some things you could do right now to help with this conflict and get your team to talk to you again?*

Katie: *I guess (without sincerity) I could apologize to them and tell them I was wrong.*

Steve: *Apologizing is a good way to begin, if it is sincere, and since you are all in this building I would suggest you do this in person. I also suggest you have a plan as to how you are going to think through the suggestions they've made for the new project and see the value in those ideas without knocking them or the people down. Do you want to try it out with me first?*

Katie: *NO, I understand and I don't mean to be like this, but I just find it difficult to listen to the entire group's ideas and to give each idea a chance. If this approach doesn't work on the first person, I will be back!*

Steve: *I know this is difficult, but what you will get out of it once you stop working against the team but with the team, is that the conflict will be reduced and you won't feel so stressed out. Let me know how it goes— I know you can do this!*

So What Transpired Here?

Katie is a Millennial who has had a very privileged, and some would say indulged, life. She does not always understand how she comes across because her experiences have told her that, while she may not be the most popular, she gets her way when she bulldozes through things. This team is not having it, and maybe for the first time in her life Katie has been unable to get her way or work the others over enough that they just give in to what she wants.

As a seasoned business professional this may be "common sense" to you and may build your case that Millennials are not mature and appear to act in ways that indicate they feel entitled, but what's in it for you is that coaching them on these behaviors and helping them to make the connection between their behavior and how people respond to them to support their development will also support your team and/or business goals.

Adultescents

Maturity can be challenging for anyone in any generation. Millennials have had many opportunities which have allowed them to postpone maturity, including the ease afforded by being able to live with their parents and receive family support. "Adultescence" is defined as a blend of "adult" and "adolescent," a childless person whose tastes and hobbies are typically associated with that of a younger person. A *New York Times* article described it as a person with teenage tastes and an adult credit card.

As applying this term to them indicates, Millennials are not maturing as quickly as the generations preceding them. They have been allowed to remain kids for such a long time that they are in no hurry to grab the reins of maturity. In the past, people moved from childhood to adolescence and from adolescence to adulthood, but today there appears to be a new intermediate phase. The years from eighteen to twenty-eight and even beyond have become a distinct and separate life stage in which people stall for a few extra years, putting off the mantel of adult responsibility because they can remain in their families' homes without embarrassment. In fact, the Great Recession has enabled this life-style. Families band together to save on expenses while Millennials struggle to find full-time meaningful work.

According to the American Sociological Association,[14] the number of twentysomethings reaching traditional marks of adulthood before age thirty—graduation, leaving home, getting a full-time job, marriage, having a baby—has dropped from 77 percent of women and 65 percent of men in 1960 to 46 percent of women and 31 percent of men in

2010. Additionally, 40 percent of those in their late twenties still receive economic support from their parents, while close to 50 percent still live at home.

Consider these other statistics:[15]

- The World Adult Kickball Association—for those over twenty-one— was launched in Washington a few years ago. Today it has more than twenty thousand registered members nationwide who pay sixty dollars apiece to belong. The annual open tournament, held in June in Centreville, Virginia, drew nearly three hundred players.

- *Business Week* reports that the Cartoon Network attracts higher ratings among viewers ages eighteen to thirty-four than CNN, MSNBC, or any other cable news channel.

- Disney World is the top adult vacation destination in the world.

- The average age of people who play video games is thirty-three, according to the Entertainment Software Association.

- Many cafes offer adult-sized peanut butter and jelly sandwiches.

A Delaware company known as the Fun Department gets paid to help corporations stage "recess" at work. Employees compete in activities that were once staples of the elementary playground, including relay races, a giant version of Yahtzee, and a version of broom hockey. Child's play among coworkers "creates happy employees and supports team-building, morale and motivation, and fun for fun's sake," says the company's marketing chief, Jayla Boire. Juvenile behavior also helps companies recruit and retain talented people, she says, because "a sense of fun" is a big draw for young prospective workers. The Fun Department uses splashy words such as "funnertainment" and "funsters."

Conversely, Boire explains, "funkillers are people who don't remember that they have a funny bone and they find it difficult to find their inner child. Our job is to 'out' the funkillers and bring them to recess."

Other tools the Fun Department uses in this mission are Silly String wars, squirt-gun games, and "the Boss Toss," in which employees catapult a stick figure that looks like an executive into a trash can.

What's Going on Here?

"There is definitely something happening," says Christopher Noxon, author of *Rejuvenile: Kickball, Cartoons, Cupcakes, and the Reinvention of the American Grown-up.*[16] Adults are turning to child's play, Noxon says, because "everything is up for grabs. Social norms have evaporated." The change is "pervasive and cross-generational." Not too long ago, society frowned on forty-year-old skateboarders or comic book collectors. "Now they are celebrated."

Noxon explains that the shift was facilitated through affluence. After all, "it's hard to nurture your inner child when you're struggling to keep food on the table." But he said other factors have fed the adult attraction to childish things—for instance, the strange and uncertain aftermath of 9/11 and looser hierarchies in the workplace. "Witness row upon row of cubicles piled high with lunchboxes, action figures and Beanie Babies." The reshaping of traditional household roles has allowed parents of both genders to identify more closely with their children, Noxon adds. And longer life spans "have kept us in tune with our childlike sides longer than ever."

A New Approach

For earlier generations of workers, an unspoken sink-or-swim approach to on-the-job training was often good enough to bring new employees up to speed. This approach may be less effective with those from the Millennial generation, a group raised with different expectations and work styles.

Millennials, possibly more than any other generation, require clear direction, guidance, and well-stated goals from their managers. This is because many Millennials have grown up in schools that use rubrics to evaluate the quality of an assignment. According to the National Education Association (NEA) website, rubrics are "scoring tools that divide an assignment into its component parts and objectives, and provide a description of what constitutes acceptable and unacceptable levels of performance for each part." In many cases, rubrics are provided to students at the time an assignment is given so they know exactly what to do to achieve a certain grade.

Most Millennials are used to well-defined assignments, clear benchmarks, and continual feedback and discussion. As such, it is a process they assume will be in place in the business world as well. The lack of success many companies have experienced in working with Millennials is the result of a collision between this generation's worldview and how most companies function.

To leverage the talents of this highly educated and goal-oriented generation, supervisors need a new approach. Rather than assuming that new workers will absorb an organization's culture without explicit discussion, proceeding in the same way previous generations have done, enlightened companies are redesigning supervisor and leadership training to accommodate the more interactive and collaborative work style of Millennials.

Managers would be well-served to understand that the young members of their workforce place more immediate demands on them than managers likely placed on their mentors. This means that managers must be prepared to spend as much time describing the task an employee is expected to complete as they spend explaining proper business behavior, such as cell phone and Internet use at work.

The new training paradigm to successfully train Millennials lies in connecting the dots. Millennials thrive on certainty and clarity. For many, ambiguity is not part of their immediate skill set, in part because this generation grew up playing video games with static rules—you knew when things changed, no surprises.

⏱ MILLENNIAL MINUTE

Communicate, communicate, communicate! Communicate in person, online, via email, texting, and by sharing interesting and relevant articles. Millennials want to know what is going on and love to learn about company metrics and customer feedback. Sharing how things are going is a great strategy to build trust. Clear expectations raise the bar, but frequent communication holds everyone to them.

• • • • • • • • • • • • • • • • • • •

Building Trust—Start with an "A"

When many baby boomers began their careers, the concept was that you have a "zero" until you have demonstrated what you can do, what skills you possess, and you begin to accumulate contributions. This was well understood, and though you may have thought your boss was a jerk, you kept your thoughts close and did the best you could. Millennials bring a different mindset as they begin their careers. They believe, as they have been told, that they are smart, competent, and that they can get results! Holding onto the concept that Millennials need to pay their dues in the same way you may have experienced is unlikely to get you the daily performance you need.

When you begin a new business relationship, try starting with an "A," 100 percent, or a perfect score. This sends the message that I believe in you, your skills, and what you bring to the job and the team. Sharing this intent with others, especially your Millennial talent, will provide you an approach that supports effective business relationships in a manner that is consistent with the paradigm of this generation. Millennials believe, as they have been taught, that they are "worthy" from the start and that they have much to contribute, even at entry-level jobs. Millennials have been **raised on praise**, so this is what they are familiar with.

Much has been written about trust and how important it is in business as well as in relationships. Millennials view trust through highly-focused lenses because their experiences growing up have shown them that not everything or everyone is as they appear. They learned that anyone can say anything they want, but integrity is about character and the way one behaves—what one does reveals the truth. The goal is to engage in two-way conversations where each person is being open and honest while maintaining a sense of decorum.

❋ *Case Study*

Here's a conversation that incorporates the trust element focusing on someone new to the company or to your team. Max is a Baby Boomer. Zoe is one of his Millennial employees and is typically rather quiet. Zoe is a wizard on the computer and in putting visual presentations together. Zoe is creative but, being on the shy, side, she does not always come forward with her ideas. But she is determined that in her upcoming meeting with her supervisor she will present her ideas about her project forcefully, especially since she expects that he may not agree with her approach. Zoe is fortunate that she has a strong relationship with her parents and they have provided her some coaching and even role-playing to help her assert herself and convince her boss why her ideas are good for the company and the client.

> **Zoe**: *Hi Max! I'm here for our one-to-one and I want to start by talking about the client presentation. I'm really excited about this project! I've worked really hard to challenge myself and I've had help and some*

ideas from the team. I really think that edgier is the way to go. The client wants something bold!

Max: *I know you feel strongly that to really capture the client's passion for this project we need to focus on edgier approaches for the presentation. But as you know, the business backdrop is challenging and we can't afford to miss the client's expectation in any way. I know we don't agree on the approach to this presentation.*

Zoe: *Yes, I feel strongly that edgier, thought-provoking, and out-of-the box would be the way to go. I know a lot has been written about how important trust is to all relationships, including the relationship between boss and employee. But trust is a two-way proposition. Max, you need to trust me and my instincts on this approach. I know you've been doing your job for years and have great instincts, but so do I. Just because I'm not "seasoned" doesn't mean I'm not correct. I want my ideas to be judged based on how good they are. I don't want my age to hold you back on how you view my ideas. As you know, I'm not typically assertive about advocating for my way, but I hope you see that I feel passionately about this approach.*

Max: *Zoe, your passion about this is energizing and I do trust you, but a lot is riding on this and we can't afford to fail. I'm concerned if the presentation is too edgy and we miss expectations, it will be hard to regroup. This is such an out-of-the box idea. What if they don't like it?*

Zoe: *Isn't there always a chance that the client won't like it? These are challenging business times, so all the more reason to try something different to capture attention; not for shock value but from the 'what would happen, what could happen' aspect.*

Max: *I applaud your enthusiasm and I especially like that you thought this through and anticipated my objections!*

Zoe: *I have an idea! What if we could find some people who have similar buying habits to our client and do a test focus group with them and see what their reactions are to our presentation?*

Max: *I think that's a good idea, but do we have time to find "some people" who would provide us with feedback that would be on par with the clients? There is not much time.*

Zoe: *Let me give it a try—I'll get on it today and will keep you posted. If* *this group doesn't find what we are proposing interesting and provocative, then we'll pull it back, as you suggested.*

Max: *Not that I don't trust your feedback, but I want to attend this pilot meeting. I will commit to staying quiet until we are finished and then ask the group questions.*

Zoe: *Great! Thanks for giving me a shot—I know this is a big stretch for you!*

Max: *Yes, it is, let's see what happens.*

So What Transpired Here?

Zoe is really finding her professional voice and is feeling more and more comfortable about asserting her ideas. Of course this is good and bad! As a manager who must count on the team to manage the enormous workload and the challenges of meeting and exceeding clients' expectations, the team's engagement and productivity is critical. Rather than viewing this as a challenge, Max sees this as an opportunity.

Max had to make a tough call with Zoe. Her ideas are great, but with the harsh business backdrop, can anyone afford to make a mistake and miss client expectations? Max allowed Zoe a "controlled" chance, which achieved a lot of good things including:

➤ Zoe is motivated to do a great job; it's very possible the client will react positively to the new ideas.

➤ Word will spread that Max is willing to try new things.

➤ Because Max trusted Zoe and did not assume that her youth means she is not ready to have great ideas, more ideas and innovations are likely to follow.

⏱ MILLENNIAL MINUTE

Trust is a powerful tool and when applied with strong business acumen, it will yield effective results!

● ● ● ● ● ● ● ● ● ● ● ● ● ● ● ● ● ●

Leading the Networked Environment*

Social, economic, environmental, and technological forces continuously transform the relationship between organizations and employees. The traditional "workplace" is disappearing, courtesy of globalization, communications, the consumerization of IT, and recent market upheavals. In its place is a "workspace" that is more social, more virtual and more mobile. This new workspace is also more transitory, as employees skeptical of lifetime employment find themselves increasingly joined by contingent staff and outsourcing partners. Also—given the ascent of a new generation of workers raised in this connected, global reality—we can no longer rely on old assumptions on how work best gets done.

The type of agility necessary to achieve breakthrough levels of innovation and growth will rely on people and the ability of the organization to leverage the network of relationships that interconnect them. Leadership teams must develop collaborative operating models responsive to market and stakeholder needs—including those of its "employees." Such transformation creates an environment where people are managed not by sight, but by trust and commitment. Here are some questions to ponder:

- How should your organization position and ready itself for change?

- What type of capabilities and collaborative operating models are needed?

- How can the strengths each generation brings be leveraged?

- How can communities and social networking contribute towards a more agile and high-performing organization?

- What role will technology play in this transformation?

- What role does trust play as the way work is accomplished shifts and changes?

* This text is from the introduction to the *E 2.0 Workshop: Organization Next*, conducted by Mike Gotta, Sarah Roberts, and Daniel Rasmus, used by courtesy of the authors.
http://www.e2conf.com/boston/conference/organization-next.php

Key Takeaways for Building Trust: Isn't That Cheating?

If you surveyed coworkers and asked them if they agreed with the statement that if someone cheats, it would erode your trust in them, most would agree. In the many corporate focus groups we facilitated, we heard, about the challenges of the multi-generations and how each generation went about getting work completed. One of those challenges was the concept of cheating—defined as deceiving someone, breaking the rules to gain advantage and somehow give yourself the upper hand. This very conversation leads to how this younger generation is so comfortable with social media that their first response is to grab their mobile device and obtain data—some of the more seasoned generations thought this was cheating! Here is how that very perception of utilizing social media can impact someone's idea of cheating.

Words with Friends has become a very popular mobile device game. It's a Scrabble-style game for your phone, anywhere, anytime! In a recent workshop we had multiple generations discussing the impact of social media and the many ways in which handheld devices have changed the way we connect and communicate. A baby boomer shared the story of his daughter consistently beating him, game after game, at Words with Friends. Not only was he older and more experienced, but he even used his pocket dictionary to play, so he really felt he had several advantages.

Guess why his daughter consistently won? She went online and used the many sites that provide however many words you want beginning and or ending with whatever letter you want! The boomer dad believed she was "cheating," but this Millennial was just using the tools and resources available at her fingertips. According to his daughter it was not "cheating" but it is interesting that a boomer would think it was. While not all Millennials agree about playing the game this way, this is a great illustration of how resetting your perspective to better understand the experiences of your Gen Y employees can provide you with a new paradigm. Since we defined cheating as breaking the rules to gain an advantage, deceiving somebody, do you think this Millennial cheated at *Words with Friends?* Many of them would think no rules were broken here. Understanding the vast options that are available online, including apps, and the entire social media spectrum, changes the way these young people view their world, their work, and how to be quick and resourceful.

This concept of using your resources as well as reaching out to social networks is how Millennials have gone to school, how they process, how they expect to work. The days of checking out books in a library to complete papers or letting your fingers walk through the card index as you searched for information, is no longer the norm or in common practice.

Rob Salkowitz, noted author and one of the first to write about the social implications of new technologies in the next generation and the impact on the workplace, shares his outlook about Millennials in the workplace and the role of collaborative technology from his book, *Generation Blend:*

> Can Millennials live without IM, blogs, and social networks at work? Of course. Will they still work for employers who don't equip them with the latest and greatest stuff to allow them to achieve the work/life integration they say they want? Some will, at least until they pay off their student loans and credit card debt, or get a better offer. However, in a competitive global environment, it's not about the minimum you can get away with; it's about the maximum you can achieve. Young workers empowered with collaborative technology can be enormous creators of value, as can workers of any age. Young workers motivated by a workplace that respects their autonomy and supports their life and work priorities will be an asset to their employers for years to come. Young workers will support management decisions and respect boundaries if organizations take the time to explain the context and rationale.

✦ 4 ✦

Helping Gen Ys to Find Their PASSION

ACUMEN: quick insight or the ability to make accurate judgments of people or situations, especially as they relate to business. Acumen *derives from* acute, *from the Latin word meaning sharpness or point.*

Acumen is a word that is broadly applied to those who "get it," those in the business environment who are savvy and understand how business gets done, not just on an operational level, but also on a relationship level. Millennials come to the workplace with strong tech skills and the ability to multitask, but they also generally come with a lack of acumen. Business acumen is typically a skill that is fine-tuned over time, so many of those just entering the professional work arena do not yet possess it, nor did the generations that came before them when they were first entered the workforce.

Effective business-acumen skills generally include a professional manner and attitude of putting the client or customer's needs first, figuring out the best thing for the team before satisfying your own needs, and using business etiquette in all types of meetings, conversations, and communications. At the foundation of this acumen is the ability to build effective business relationships. Increasing your ability to communicate with your Millennials is a critical step in engaging them. Likewise, once you are able to engage or connect with them, your ability to effectively communicate increases. But here is the curious intersection: if we could quickly increase the ability of our team's Millennials to make better judgments about people and have greater depth of insight about situations, business solutions, and opportunities, what would that be worth to you and the business? And what would it look like, on your part, to coach these key business skills?

As the team's leader, your Millennials are looking to you to be a model of business acumen, as well as to coach them on what they need to do differently to obtain the level of savvy that will help them as they develop their skill set. Millennials are very interested in building their array of skills, and you will find them most receptive when they understand how your coaching will help them learn business acumen.

Coaching for the Development of Business Acumen

At the foundation of having acumen is an employee's understanding of what's expected about performance, attire and demeanor, and business etiquette. These may all be common sense to you, but when queried, Millennials often complain that they don't understand what's expected on the job and when they go off path, they feel they are chastised for trying to figure it out on their own! The following are coaching opportunities that support developing business acumen.

Performance expectations—Looking from a daily to weekly perspective, what are the key job responsibilities? Utilize the "a day in the life" format for an employee/contractor and describe what it would look like. Within this conversation is a good place to share things about the culture. For example, "We've made a commitment to return internal emails within twenty-four hours," or any other specific and important cultural norm.

Punctuality/attendance—This is one of the biggest push-backs employers manage with Millennials. "What difference does it make what time I get to the office, if I get my work done?" Millennials come at this concept from a totally different paradigm. Having "face time" does not have the same importance or meaningfulness to them as it may have to you. Here's a great place to clarify expectations. When you provide the "why" for them here, it will help them better understand what a difference this makes.

Professional attire and demeanor—Every office has official rules about dress, but not typically about demeanor—in other words, how we act when we are working, the rules of the road that you probably won't find in an employee handbook. "Since our department requires that we have to meet with customers, we don't wear super casual clothes, because we are representing the brand." Let your team know what is acceptable and what is not. When you assume they know, nobody wins.

Business etiquette—What are the rules of etiquette that apply to your work world? Do they include the common courtesies that are shared when using the break room, for example picking up after yourself and not bringing foods with intense aromas to microwave? Is it everyone's job to acknowledge and help customers find what they need, even if you are not on the front line?

Improving Communication by Understanding Gen Y's Work Habits

One of the quickest methods of improving communication with Millennials is to understand their work habits and apply them to improve communication effectiveness between you and them. In order to communicate at the most helpful level, understanding another's perspective is critical. The chart on the next page shows behaviors and characteristics of Millennials that are not always understood, a little about why these behaviors exist, and suggestions to make a stronger connection.

MILLENNIAL MINUTE

When texting, Millennials use as few words and letters as possible. Their economy of words is amazing, yet they have a high need for clear, specific communication in their work life. For example: K (okay), g2g (got to go), IMHO (in my humble opinion), BRB (be right back), ROFL (rolling on floor laughing), BTW (by the way), and SUP (what's up). Is less really more?

Improving Communication by Understanding Gen Ys' Work Ethic

"Work ethic" (first used in 1951) is often defined as a dedication to work or the belief in the moral value of hard work. *Work ethic* is a set of values based on hard work and diligence. It is also a belief in the

Behavior	Why it's so	Try to:
Experiential learning	Millennials have learned by doing and interacting and from participating in multi-player games, computer simulations, and social networks where there is little penalty for trial-and-error learning.	Give brief but clear instructions about a task or assignment; let them try it out, but be prepared to answer questions so they will be quickly on the road to productivity.
Results-Oriented Behavior	Millennials are interested in processes that work to speed up their interactions. They don't like to waste their time if they believe they know a better, more effective way to get the task completed.	Allow them to come up with a better way, with the caveat that they need to demonstrate why their new way is better, how it saves time, energy, and resources and what the impact might be on other departments or other processes.
Customization	As Millennials were growing up, they were given many choices about products as well as services, including the way they like to learn. They have customized their ring tones to know instantly who is calling and are used to making things their own. They are happy to share how they like to learn and how they prefer to receive feedback. When they are allowed to make things their own, they are more engaged and productive.	Ask them how they like to learn. Also ask how they like to receive feedback and how they like to communicate. The suggestion is not that they get to have everything their way, but as you better understand their habits, they will respond in kind with increased productivity and effectiveness and understand how to best communicate with you.
Impatience	Millennials are accustomed to speed. They become impatient when things or people do not go as fast they would like.	Ask them how fast they like to work, and help them to understand that things will go even faster as they become more proficient. Caution: because of someone's impatience or lack of detailed instruction, they may not have heard or understood an entire assignment or task. So in the beginning, ask them to repeat back to you what they heard and what they will be doing. These are just "training wheels" and will fall away once they become more proficient and confident.

ability of hard work to enhance a person's character. This workplace concept is founded upon the Puritan work ethic. The necessity for hard work was thought to promote a person's calling and success was a sign of personal salvation, thus work ethic became the behavioral norm for most Americans. But this concept does not resonate with either Millennials or most Gen Xers. The new definition of work ethic is figuring out how to work smarter, not harder! With the amazing array of tech tools, continual connectedness, and the ability to text, tweet, or ping a friend, ideas, solutions, and information are fast, easy, and right now—so why wouldn't you use them?

One of the comments I often hear in workshops dealing with Millennials concerns their lack of work ethic. Research indicates that this "entitled generation" thinks they will arrive on the work scene and—voilà!—instantly receive exciting, meaningful, and challenging work to do. The POTENTIAL chapter highlighted that having unwarranted entitlement is not how Millennials perceive themselves and their world—they just know what they've experienced in their lives. For many, this has been parents, families, teachers, and coaches smoothing the way of obstacles, making things easier for them. This has had a big impact on the concept of work ethic and the way they perceive "work."

Millennials are constantly looking at ways to work smarter, not harder, figuring out the path of least resistance. This is the model they've grown up with; this is what they know. Your idea of work ethic might be getting to the office early and staying late. It might include asking others how you can help them and always being available. It might be canceling days off or vacations to manage the business needs at hand. Millennials value work–life balance, so they have a different perspective.

⏰ MILLENNIAL MINUTE

Did one of your young employees break one of those unwritten company rules? Can you believe they were talking in the lunch-room about last night's date and they shared intimate details OUT LOUD? Yes, they are doing what they are accustomed to, saying what's on their mind. YOU will need to provide those unwritten rules to help them with their brand. You know they love when you talk about THEIR brand! This will help them avoid making that same mistake again. Just like work ethic, they need feedback and coaching to help them better align with the expectations of their behavior.

Closing the Work-Ethic Standards Gap

The first place to start is to be clear about your work-ethic standards. Is it all about the quality of the work, or is it important for you to know how the work gets completed, the process? Is face time something you measure as a way to determine work ethic? A Millennial might say that someone can be in the office early, stay late, and look busy without doing any work at all! This is why being clear about how work is judged is critical to clarifying this perceived lack of a work ethic, meaning a standard set of values and moral behavior that includes hard work and diligence.

Millennials want to find the answers themselves; they don't want to be spoon-fed, but they expect you to be electronically available if they have a question or need further clarification. This dynamic can create conflict, as it seems to be a conundrum: you don't want me to spoon-feed you, because you like to learn and discover on your own, but you do want me to be instantly available in the event that you have a question, because you want the answer right now!

This conundrum also impacts the quality of work ethic. You may believe that a part of having a good work ethic is being able to work independently. Millennials do work independently, but they need to know they can contact you by text or email. Their position is that through your response to their text they are able to quickly move forward and on to the next work item. For this text or email, they simply want an answer; they do not believe any social niceties need to be attached to this quick, info-loaded communication. This is their perception of a correct work ethic—completing a task by using tech tools and their team to instantly collaborate, ask questions, obtain data, and move forward.

Controlling Controllables

Part of understanding the impact of business acumen is knowing what to focus on and what is not worth the time. We can control some areas of business, such as spending, labor, and energy use. But we can't control others, such as the price of raw materials, acts of nature, the weather, or how others behave. (There is some gray area here, but you get the point!) Spending your time as well as your Millennials' time on things that are not controllable is an ineffective use of time and energy. Having the business acumen to know the difference is an important role you can fulfill for your Millennials.

Perhaps it is the exuberance of youth (though our research indicates it is actually part of the Millennial mindset) to take a look at what exists and want to make it better. Remember, we've told them that their opinion matters, so they expect to be taken seriously. But helping them focus on the things that they can control within *their* world will be far more satisfying. This is not to say that making changes to old processes or ideas is not good business. But all that energy and focus would be better served focusing on the things they *can* control.

Every organization needs to determine what is controllable and what is not. Can you control who your employees are, or who your customers are? Can you control what your competitors provide? Help your team be more effective and spend their energy on the things that *can* be controlled. Here are a few ideas of things that can be controlled:

➢ Promote a positive frame of mind or attitude.

➢ Ensure that the environment is open and encouraging rather than punitive and threatening.

➢ Consider how much feedback and communication is provided and heard.

➢ Set clear expectations.

➢ Get back to your team on a timely basis so they can move forward.

⏱ MILLENNIAL MINUTE

Being consistent about the way you lead and supervise will serve you in the long run. Altering or changing the rules in the middle of the game creates inconsistencies, which many Millennials will challenge by calling you out about *why* the rules shifted.

● ● ● ● ● ● ● ● ● ● ● ● ● ● ● ● ● ●

Cultivating Professionalism

As you coach your Millennials to enhance their business acumen, select which area will be of greatest value. The following chart gives some areas that have consistently been highlighted by savvy managers as they review behaviors in which Millennials can often improve to become more professional in the workplace as well as with clients, customers, and coworkers.

Improving Behavior to be More Professional in the Workplace

Behavior Goal	How to Achieve This	Why Goal is Important
Appear more professional by the way you dress	What needs to change to appear more professional? Clothes that present a more business like image. Perhaps fewer jeans with holes, more jackets.	Clients and customers judge the brand based on how staff appear. Meeting clients' expectations by how we appear is the first step in gaining their confidence and sustaining their business.
Speak without excessive use of acronyms and jargon	What do they need to alter to become more professional? Save "dude" for friends, not everyone understands that "dude" is a multipurpose greeting in Gen Y culture.	Traditionalists, and frequently Baby Boomers as well, actually find a "dude" greeting disrespectful. Not everyone needs a "yes, sir" or "no, ma'am" response, but keeping "dude" for your close friends is advisable!
Be a better listener	Being a good listener is an agreed-upon quality of good business acumen. This is done by focusing on the speaker and, having your body language also be "listening" by leaning in slightly and providing positive visual signs such as nodding.	No matter which generation you identify with, we all want to be heard. Customers' and clients' perception of a company's brand is highly influenced by having staff that listen and respond appropriately.
Ask questions	Open-ended questions that require in-depth and meaningful answers usually invite the listener to speak and share what is on their mind.	When you get others to talk about themselves, they perceive YOU to be a good conversationalist!
Be aware of voice tone	The tone of our voice sends a strong message along with our words and body language. If others perceive that we have a "tone" (attitude!), they are more likely to become defensive and that can make things more difficult to manage.	Present a calm nature when things are shared to indicate that you are listening and open to hearing what they have to say.
Be more accountable	Take responsibility for your actions and initiate strong follow-ups. Many savvy professionals view being accountable as a mature and sought-after attribute.	Millennials have taken a "hit" in popular media for being entitled and unaccountable for their actions. They may require clarification on what this means. Be as clear and specific as you can on what accountability looks and sounds like in their job and in your work environment.

Behavior Goal	How to Achieve This	Why Goal is Important
Project appreciation	Constantly complaining about the things that you don't enjoy significantly drives down how you are viewed professionally. Strive for an attitude of gratitude!	Accustomed to being honest and less filtered than seasoned employees, when Gen Ys sound whiney it projects immaturity and reduces the perceived value they bring to the department and the team.

🕐 **MILLENNIAL MINUTE**

George Orwell, eminent author, said: "Each generation imagines itself to be more intelligent than the one that went before it, and wiser than the one that comes after it." Do you think Orwell was correct?

* * * * * * * * * * * * * * * * * *

Fear of Failure

When you've been raised on praise, as so many Millennials have experienced, it can clash with the realities of the workplace, where a different perspective about how important you are to the team or company may be held. One lesson that many Millennials haven't learned is that failure is part of the process of learning and gaining experience. There are fringe benefits to failure. Acting out of self-interest, as they have been taught to do, and feeling entitled may not serve them as effectively as it has during their growing-up years.

The older Millennials, especially those who graduated from college in 2007–2012, have been significantly impacted by the Great Recession. They have taken on college debt and, when unable to find suitable employment, have made decisions about their lives based on these tough realities.

Consider that:

- 2 percent of Millennials have put off having a baby due to financial worries.

- Only 58 percent of Millennials consistently pay their bills on time.

- 20 percent say they've postponed marriage due to financial reasons.

- There has been a 35 percent increase in average college debt since 1996 (the average Millennial college debt is $23,000).

- 24 percent have moved back with parents at least once since moving out to save money.[17]

Some would argue that because this generation has such a strong safety net, they are comfortable still living with their parents, and also that having such a strong support structure has allowed them to prolong growing up and becoming fully independent. That all may be true and is manifested in the numerous options these younger workers have. Past generations may have felt fortunate to have any job—sweeping, cleaning, or manual labor—as long as they received a regular paycheck. This is no longer the prevalent view and with continued parental financial support, not having to accept an undesirable job prolongs the dependence on family support.

One of the points of Relationship Leadership coaching is to encourage Millennials to try new skills, to stretch themselves, and assure them that if things do not go as well as they wanted they can learn from those "mistakes" and apply what's been learned as they go forward. Creating a culture where learning is encouraged and in which mistakes will not become a public embarrassment will go miles in addressing their fear of failure.

MILLENNIAL MINUTE

Millennials do take work seriously and are trying to understand what's expected, what work ethic means to you as their supervisor or manager, what's needed, and how to behave in today's workplace. Penelope Trunk writes a nationally syndicated column helping Millennials use social networking to build these necessary skills, as well as professional relationships.

Here is the link to her site: http://blog.penelopetrunk.com.

Connecting: Northrop Grumman

Northrop Grumman's ConnectIng program is run by employees, for employees and its aim is to retain recently hired and highly skilled engineers. The all-volunteer team organizes social networking, community outreach and professional development activities across twenty-six geographic regions. In the past three years, more than 15 percent of Northrop Grumman employees have participated in more than 1,000 events.

The program also focuses on providing education about the business, industry trends, and relevant career planning information. It also aims to provide frequent interaction with senior executives who provide guidance on career paths to new hires. [18]

Key Takeaways for Helping Gen Ys
to Develop Business Acumen

Millennials find decision-making challenging because they are afraid of making a mistake; they would rather check in with someone like their boss than make a misstep. They need help to overcome this in order to have a more professional business attitude.

Millennials are accustomed to working on team projects, as the "team approach" was part of the learning process and carried throughout all their educational experiences. They need help in learning to work more independently to have confidence to make individual decisions.

✦ Millennials favor a corporate culture of inclusion and tolerance. They need to understand that this is a generational difference and should be patient with older generations who have grown up with a "top-down" management style. They may need to be coached to understand that there is some difference between a new employee and an experienced team member

✦ Millennials want to work in an environment that actively promotes racial and cultural diversity. A lot can be learned and applied from these values.

In a recent Roper Survey, when Millennials were asked for the major cause of problems in the United States, they answered "selfishness." They might be coached to understand that their attitudes and behavior can be perceived as self-centered.

Millennials are also referred to as "Gen Why," and this generation has a high need to know why decisions are made a certain way, *why* you asked them to do something a certain way, and *why* something is important.

✦ 5 ✦

Supporting Gen Ys to Find Their PASSION

PASSION: an intense desire or enthusiasm for something; an object of enthusiasm; an outburst of emotion.

Millennials have been raised to feel enormous passion—for their environment, helping their communities, and becoming productive Global Citizens. Millennials have not known a world without the Internet (only those born in the 80s were without it as children), and they've been plugged in from an early age. Many had toy cell phones and play computers when they were just toddlers. They are accustomed to having 24/7 access to world events and what's happening in their online social networks. They can't fathom a world without instant access and information.

As they were growing up, parents tried to support all of their passions—whether it was soccer, karate, computers, or community volunteer work—and found classes or coaches to aid in this development while encouraging them to learn, stretch, and grow. This "follow your passion" concept moves with Millennials as they enter the workplace, especially as they navigate their way to finding careers that support what they love. An additional message that they heard was that work should be fun, because when you do what you love, what you are passionate about, it will be enjoyable. Though it may not be your take or experience that work is or can be fun, Millennials will frequently have this expectation.

What does passion mean in the workplace? Millennials are ready to take on challenges and embrace them. For them, boring is bad. They want their day to have a change of pace and don't want to be ignored or have their contributions trivialized. Channeling their collective passion can bring positive changes to your workplace and the communities you serve. In order to quickly accomplish this, Millennials require feedback and ongoing coaching. As you continue to build a relationship, coaching and feedback are key tools to utilize. Let's explore how to encourage passion in your work environment beginning with some effective and easy to follow coaching guidelines.

⏱ *Millennial Minute*

Millennials are inclusive, not typically judgmental about race, ethnicity, gender, or sexual preference. This strengthens their ability to work in groups and with others individually, as they don't judge based on external characteristics. They also do not think they should be judged on these characteristics. Their tattoos, body piercing, or hair color are just part of their brand, and Millennials don't understand why they should change that. One Millennial, when asked about whether or not they would cover their tattoo to obtain a position they wanted, looked at the interviewer and asked: "Would you color your hair pink if you wanted to fit into my team?"

● ● ● ● ● ● ● ● ● ● ● ● ● ● ● ● ● ● ●

Coaching Passion Guidelines

Coaching is a foundational skill for being an effective leader and goes a long way in creating a productive working relationship with the Millennials on your team. Coaching is a much-discussed topic as it relates to Millennials. Coaching is essential to having the feedback that enables continued good performance and to correcting what doesn't work. Effective coaching can build confidence and help employees to "find their passion," to reach their potential, something which is near and dear to the Millennial's heart. Ongoing feedback and coaching, assuming it is done in a positive way that does not erode self-esteem, demonstrates to your younger workers, that you do care about the work quality, employee development and, when utilized consistently, that you care about them! Coaching is a method to encourage their passions that relate to the work at hand.

Millennials are accustomed to a coaching relationship as many had coaches not only in the sports areas while they played soccer, baseball, or any of the sporting activities they participated in, but also for math, reading, and college admissions to help them find the right campus. Their college admissions coach began the relationship typically during sophomore year in high school. Oftentimes teachers and other adults took on this "coaching role" creating a generation expecting performance feedback.

We live in a world filled with tons of data and content which we are challenged to sift through each day. We are so bombarded by messages and information that we need to be able to understand our priorities and figure out what's important to know, and what is not. So in the spirit of simplicity, here is a coaching model that is deceptively simple, but effective. The goal is to provide ongoing coaching and feedback. The P.D.F. acronym is to help you remember these simple steps:

Prepare

What is the purpose of the coaching?

When is the best time to coach this person?

Why did you select to coach now?

Discuss

Explain your perspective

Listen to their response

Ask for their ideas

Discuss options

Agree on a solution

Follow-Up

How did it go?

Were the desired results achieved?

✳ *Case Study*

The following case study is an example of what a brief coaching conversation would sound like, to support, develop and encourage passion. Julia is a Gen X supervisor and is just starting to understand the return on investment as she makes better connections with the

Millennials on her team. Julia, like many Gen Xers, believes that this younger generation has been coddled and hand held. As she has learned more about why this is so, Julia has been more effective at building relationships that are having a positive impact on the business. Julia feels that she is investing time, not just expending energy, and knows that an employee who is passionate about her or his work contributes to the company at higher levels. Here is Julia's conversation with Scott, a Millennial who has been challenged to work independently, but is very coachable and open to direction.

Julia: *"Scott, I wanted to share some feedback about your preliminary report, is this a good time?"*

Scott: *"Sure, you know how much I value feedback!"*

Julia: *"Right. I reviewed the report and I see where you're headed, but you had said you had so much to contribute, I don't see that information in here."*

Scott: *"Well, I started on the project and wanted to meet your deadline, and then I was distracted by some other work, so I just realized it was due and did the best I could to get it done quickly."*

Julia: *"I appreciate the respect for deadlines, but this was not what I was expecting. What happened to all that energy and enthusiasm in obtaining the data and taking it to the next level of how this content will impact our customers? What happened to your interest in this report? Why didn't you just let me know you needed more time or even time to continue discussing how to proceed?"*

Scott: *"Well, I thought the deadline was the most important thing. I didn't want to disappoint you. I guess I should have just been honest and come back for more guidance. I know you've been wanting me to work more independently and I was trying to do that, I guess I should have asked more questions."*

Julia: *"I appreciate you trying to work more independently, that is one of our goals, but let's use our time now to take another look at the report and discuss how you can get back on track and really take this report to the next level."*

Scott: *"That would be great, I do have some ideas, and I do feel strongly that we can really impress the client. How about we start with the report outcomes?"*

So What Transpired Here?

Julia, via her coaching conversation, was able to put Scott back on track for this project and provide feedback about deadlines (important but not at the sacrifice of the project's integrity). Though she appreciated that he tried to incorporate his previous feedback about working more independently, she made sure to let him know that when clarification is needed, he should ask. This coaching conversation sends many messages: I care about you, I care about our work, I'm investing in your understanding and development, and I will continue to provide feedback as needed. Julia called Scott on his proclaimed enthusiasm, his passion for doing a great job and including his many ideas. As you coach regularly, your Gen Y employees will see the pattern of questions you will ask and they know they will need to be a part of any solutions that need to be accomplished. They are accustomed to their parents, teachers, coaches, and tutors providing coaching, so they are "coachable" and responsive.

⏱ *MILLENNIAL MINUTE*

In a recent survey, 47 percent of Millennials said that it's important that the company they work for offer sabbatical leaves and that such perks boost commitment and performance. Of those who've taken the opportunity for a leave, 53 percent use the time to explore their "passions" such as taking advantage of opportunities for volunteering or doing other charitable work.[19]

How Passion Gets Results!

In the research we conducted via focus groups, in person, and by utilizing online feedback, the Millennials we talked with were clear—they want to bring all they have to a job, do good work, and feel connected to a team. This connection is the often talked about workplace "engagement." There are many tools and surveys that organizations employ to determine their levels of employee engagement.

This process has been going on for years. For example, Gallup's research into employee engagement at work has been going on for more than thirty years of in-depth, behavioral economic research involving more than seventeen million employees. This research has appeared in business and scientific publications, including the *Journal of Applied Psychology* and the *Harvard Business Review,* and in bestselling books *First, Break All the Rules,* by Marcus Buckingham and Curt Coffman, and *12: The Elements of Great Managing,* by Rodd Wagner and James K. Harter.

Though this research is not new and does not focus specifically on Millennials, their findings align with what Millennials say are key to supporting their passion and obtaining the best results.

Ten Behaviors for Encouraging Millennials' Passion

As you work to build effective business relationships, encouraging their passionate interests is an effective method to increase motivation and commitment. These are ten areas you can coach to support engaging that passion in the workplace, thereby creating more effective and productive employees.

1. Millennials respond favorably to **encouragement**, as they are accustomed to collaborative relationships with their parents, teachers, and coaches. Some Millennials have a fear of failure, so they are afraid to stretch out too far, not wanting to disappoint. Millennials continually ask the question, "What's in it for me?" They respond favorably when they understand what it takes to meet or exceed the expected results. For example, Quinn is a Millennial who is bright, articulate and, when focused, produces great business results. Quinn's boss Joel values "self-starters" and feels that having to encourage and coddle this generation is indulgent. Because of this, he would seldom provide positive coaching and encouragement. During one particularly frustrating day, Joel called Quinn in to his office and asked her what she wanted from him, as her supervisor. Quinn shared that she just needed some feedback once a week or so, and encouragement about the things that were working, as well as those which were not. Once Joel tried this, he was amazed at how much more productive Quinn was, and really began to value what encouragement and feedback means to this generation. Once Millennials receive consistent encouragement and coaching, they will become loyal and highly motivated employees.

2. **Ask "How do you like to be coached?"** This can save a lot of time in the long run when you understand their perspective. Try not to get

hung-up on the "why is it always about THEM" mindset. For example, when Joe (a seasoned manager) asked his Millennial employee Marc how he liked to be coached, Marc responded that what he wanted was a quick email or text back to answer his questions so he could move forward. Marc also asked if he and Joe could have about fifteen minutes of time every other week to have a more in-depth conversation, an opportunity for Marc to ask questions and check in with Joe. This generation is used to customization in so many aspects of their lives and the "customization" Marc was asking for is easy, doable, and will not consume much time. When you consider how they like to be coached and merge that with how you like to communicate, you will come up with a comfortable approach that works for everyone. Millennials thrive on continual coaching and constructive feedback. They will quickly respond to guidance and apply it to their responsibilities. But without that kind of interaction, they will languish.

3. **Declare your intentions.** Millennials want to know that you have their best interest at heart, just like their parents, teachers, and coaches. This is especially important when you are asking them to do tasks and projects that they may not understand. For example, to help them see how things fit together and what's in it for them, you could say something such as: "My intention is that this project be the best possible, and your ability to develop the client presentation gives YOU good visibility, which is good for our team." Declaring your intentions in a clear and specific way not only shows your Gen Y employees that you are supporting their career, it also allows for the relationship-style focus that is appealing to this generation.

4. **Clarify boundaries.** Millennials have grown up in a world without boundaries. They can connect online with people from all over the planet and they can use the Internet to obtain information on just about anything. They are comfortable asking anyone questions, regardless of job title or authority, and they view their world as a woven tapestry, not as time periods divided into work, play, and socializing. The line between work and play is merged for Millennials. In a recent meeting in a traditional Fortune 100 company, a newly-hired Millennial employee asked one of the visiting executives why someone on the team was promoted over someone else. Was this a good question? It might have been, depending on

the situation, but in that forum it was out-of-bounds. To the executive, this Millennial looked naive and immature. This new hire needed coaching to understand why it was an inappropriate question in that situation. For previous generations, there were very clear social boundaries. There was a rank and file perspective in the workplace and you knew your place, like in the military, where roles were clearly defined. Providing clear expectations is critical. Lay out the rules with regard to Internet and mobile phone usage, dress, office and meeting demeanor, and other business protocols. It will eliminate confusion and frustration.

5. **Be Consistent.** Remember that Millennials pay very close attention to consistency in actions and words in the work environment. For example, inconsistency is also likely to erode credibility and hurt working relationships. One could argue that it's not just Millennials who spot inconsistencies! However, because they are blind to hierarchy and believe every colleague is basically a peer, they will call out hypocrisy when they see it. Unlike previous generations, Millennials can (and do!) broadcast their displeasure via their social networks, and they are not the least bit hesitant to share perceived injustices or major inconsistencies.

6. **Be available.** Great leaders are coaches who let their team know they are available. Figure out what the best ways for you to be available are. Millennials often just need a quick answer via email or text, or a response such as "yes, this is on the right track, keep working!" or provide with a referral in another department so they can continue working on their task.

7. **Build relationships.** Good coaches know their people. By being around them, they find out who does what well and who needs attention when. By watching what they do and listening to what they say, they can identify the real issues on the front lines.

8. **Walk the talk.** Lead by example. Millennials will model their behavior on what they want and choose. They stay focused on performance and show their team what's important by what they pay attention to.

9. **Celebrate success.** Good coaches give praise and recognition to individuals and teams as they are working towards a goal. Positive and frequent celebrations provide motivation and direction.

10. **Say thanks.** Great leaders take time to show their appreciation for a job well done. They recognize the power of a sincere thank-you.

How Do You Know If Your Message Was Delivered?

ASK for a quick replay of their understanding. This becomes more important when the message you are delivering has more constructive content. We all like to hear what's working more than what is not, but Millennials are coachable, especially when they feel comfortable and trust you. The performance benefits all come back to you and your team—engaged workers go the extra mile.

⏱ *MILLENNIAL MINUTE*

Millennials feel that work should be more enjoyable. Form a small task force and ask your Millennials to come up with three or four ideas that could make YOUR work environment more satisfying and pleasant. Let the task force know if there is a budget, or if these ideas can proceed without budgetary impact.

● ● ● ● ● ● ● ● ● ● ● ● ● ● ● ● ● ●

Managing Beyond the iFF Factor (the "I" Focus Filter)

Much has been written about the narcissistic tendencies of the Millennials. One of the factors impacting this is that 25 percent of Millennials were raised as only children. By definition, that means that one-quarter of this population were often the center of their family's universe.

While many of these only children will tell you that there is a great deal of responsibility that comes with this, because they don't have to share their parents' time, money, or resources with siblings, they are getting a larger slice of the pie!

As you engage and lead the Millennials on your team, look beyond the iFF ("I" Focus Filter). Yes, they do want to know from the beginning "What's in It for ME" (WIIFM), but as a generation that has been brought up with a great deal of focus on the "i," their filtering systems may be different than yours. Though the "i" in Apple products was born from the "i" association with the Internet, it has come to represent a generation that is focused on themselves.

Millennials will take responsibility for their success and failure, but they want to do it on their own terms. To discover what those terms include, try asking:

- What do you think your strengths are?
- How do these strengths help our team?
- How do these strengths help our clients or customers?
- What are some areas you would like to improve?
- What are your ideas about improving some of our processes and systems?
- What would be a good way to be accountable for this task or project?

Just So You Know—No Sandwich, Please!

When providing feedback, Millennials want you to be clear and direct. The famous "sandwich technique" of giving some negative feedback sandwiched between two positives is not preferred. When you have something negative to share, do so in a nonthreatening way and when you have something positive, just say it!

The Role of Social Media

Social media has played an integral role in the lives of Millennials. As the first generation to have the Internet, their worldview is seen through a global perspective. The tools and resources they have known since birth, such as social media, are simply a part of what they know, like air or water, and they assume they will always be there.

Some of the ways companies are connecting Gen Y's passion and their understanding of social media include:

- developing internal "wikis" to help all employees understand the words, acronyms, products, processes, and systems unique to the organization.
- creating internal profile sites that share professional information that can be sorted by hobbies, schools attended, affiliated community organizations, allowing people to quickly connect whether they are on the same company property or across the country or the world
- providing accessible internal ambassadors who support new hires as they acclimate to the company. (Some companies use the format of

live, chat based help for external customer support and many are adapting this format for new hire training.)

The impact of the Internet is still being felt in business as well as in society. It has fundamentally changed the way people do business, view business, obtain information, and even how they *think*. Remember when encyclopedias were the source of data? How many times a day do you "Google" or go to Wikipedia in search of information? Several colleges have even introduced classes on best social media practices, preparing students for potential careers as digital strategists.

There are various statistics that account for social media usage and effectiveness for individuals worldwide. Some of the most recent statistics are as follows:[20]

- 62 percent of adults worldwide now use social media.

- Social networking is the most popular online activity, with 22 percent of time online spent on sites like Facebook, Twitter, and Pinterest.

- Brazil has the highest online friends—an average of 481 per user.

- Japan has the lowest average online friends—an average of just 29 friends per user.

- YouTube is the second largest search engine in the world.

- 42 percent of mobile users share multimedia via Facebook.

- Google+ is the second most-used social network for sharing multimedia content from a mobile device (10 percent).

- Smartphone owners now spend as much time using social networking apps such as Twitter and Facebook as they do playing games.

- In Q1 2012, users logged an average of 24 minutes per day using social apps (on phone), with 24 minutes being spent on gaming apps.

- There were around 100 billion smartphone application sessions during Q1 2012.

- Users log an average of 77 minutes per day using apps on their smartphone.

  Facebook statistics:

- 137.6 million unique visitors per month (in the United States alone).

- 7:45:49 = time spent per person per month on Facebook.

- 54 percent of monthly users access it via a mobile device.

- Facebook has 901 million monthly active users.

- If Facebook were a country it would be the world's third largest in terms of population; that's more than the United States.

The main increase in social media has been Facebook. It was ranked as the number one social networking site. Approximately 100 million users access this site through their mobile phone. According to Nielsen, global consumers spend more than six hours per week on social networking sites. "Social Media Revolution" produced by *Socialnomics* author Erik Qualman contains numerous statistics on Social Media including the fact that 93 percent of businesses use it for marketing. In an effort to supplant Facebook's dominance, Google launched Google+ in the summer of 2011.

Social media is a new frontier and, as such, is still uncharted territory. Where it will go, how fast it will get there, and how it will continue to permeate business around the globe is still to be seen. Seth Godin, noted author, writes about the post-industrial revolution, the way ideas spread, marketing, and leadership. Seth says: "Marketing is no longer about the stuff that you make, but about the stories you tell."

⏱ *MILLENNIAL MINUTE*

Millennials started online social networks. Think about how you can leverage social networking in the workplace to encourage team collaboration and knowledge sharing. Imagine all the great benefits that social networking can provide to your team. Social networking is a form of transparency. You get to "see" the other people in the company and learn about them before meeting them or talking to them.

• • • • • • • • • • • • • • • • • • • •

Ways That Businesses Can Engage Millennials' Passions

Looking at ways to engage Millennial passion is not only a good employee development practice, it's good business. The team at ERA Real Estate is one of the important business groups that have taken a very serious look at how to actively recruit Gen Y talent and the impact that they could have as they bring their skills, their technical and social networking knowledge to the industry.

Generation Y: Rethinking Recruiting

by Charlie Young

Read how Charlie Young, President and CEO, ERA Real Estate, is proactively rethinking about Generation Y in the following recruiting effort:

When it comes to maintaining a competitive edge, there is a big difference between recognizing a need and actually doing something about it. Many people in the real estate industry know that the average age of today's real estate professional is fifty-six. With many owners and agents nearing retirement, ERA Real Estate recognized the need to prepare our brokers to bring the next generation of sales professionals on board in order to keep their companies successful. To better understand how best to bring Gen Y into the field, we conducted a comprehensive study culminating in the publication of an industry report that provides our customers—our brokers—with the knowledge and insights they needed to recruit Gen Y.

Our biggest finding was that there was some low hanging fruit in terms of who to target: Millennials are twice as likely to be interested in a real estate career if they know an agent their age or have previously worked on commission, so focusing on those populations can increase recruiting success.

We also learned that, as a profession, real estate has a lot to offer Millennials. Our report identified four key messages about a career in real estate that resonate with Gen Y:

- Be in the know: real estate agents develop extensive networks, which they like

- Get the best of both worlds: in real estate you can be in charge of your own career, but have the support of a broker

- Never a dull day: multi-tasking and working on a range of projects is appealing to Gen Y

- Emotional benefits: real estate professionals help build communities; help families find homes

The truth is Gen Y will change how the real estate business is run. We will see that play out in recruiting techniques, message development, value proposition, and even the evolution of business models. Millennials also have a great deal to offer us: they are very technologically savvy so it is likely they will bring new efficiencies and new ways of doing business to the industry. The synergies to be realized are exciting to consider and I look forward to this inevitable evolution of our industry.

Providing Career Support: To facilitate getting new recruits paid within the first thirty to sixty days, several brokers are focusing their new agents on lines of business that close more quickly. Douglas Van Nortwick with ERA Sellers, Buyers and Associates in El Paso, Texas, funnels his younger agents into roles that support military clientele who need to move quickly which gets them closing new home deals without much prospecting. Eddie Wilder, with ERA Wilder Realty in Sumter, S.C., puts his younger agents on a government HUD account which consists of a book of business that averages about forty listings at any given time.

Agent Succession/Mentoring Relationships: Bill Hurt, with ERA Shields in Colorado Springs, used an agent succession model to transition a retiring agent's book of business to a new agent. While primarily used to transition business to experienced agents, this model is easily adapted to create graduated compensation schedules for new Gen Y agents.

Using Social Recruiting: ERA Wilder Realty in Sumter, S.C., conducted a Facebook advertising campaign to test recruiting messages on the social networking platform. Over the three-week test period, engagement within the platform was high, evidenced by a high click through rate to the broker's Facebook page, a 90 percent increase in likes, more than twice the number of active users and nearly forty times the number of Facebook page views during the test.

Expected Outcomes: We are optimistic about what the future will bring as our brokers proactively recruit under this new paradigm and vision that reflects current and continuing demographic drivers. We know that as Millennials become a larger part of our business model, both as agents and customers, the results will benefit all.

Key Takeaways for Encouraging Gen Ys' Passion for Their Work

To determine if your company is moving toward being Millennial friendly to encourage their loyalty and enjoyment of and commitment toward their work, ask the following questions:

1. *Does your company support partner mentoring, where younger workers are teamed with experienced workers so that they can exchange and share expertise about technology and critical tribal knowledge?*

   Millennials are not satisfied with being the "mentee," they want to be full partners and contribute to this mentoring relationship by sharing their expertise. They will reject the paradigm that mentoring should be one-way.

2. *Does your company help new employees understand the unwritten rules of the road?*

   Millennials have grown up with a different set of boundaries and may not intuitively understand the lines between work and play, or how to treat employees, customers, and clients in a business setting. Millennials don't see the boundaries between work and play— it's all connected, and differentiating it seems odd.

3. *Does your company cultivate professionalism by clearly defining it?*

   For example, does your company have guidelines describing appropriate professional attire and cell phone use? Have you articulated what it means to be accountable? As members of the Rubric Generation, Millennials respond when they know what good, very good, and excellent performance standards include.

4. *Do your employees consider your company transparent?*

   Are they informed about its mission, goals, and objectives? Do they understand how the business works and how all the elements and processes connect?

5. *Does your work environment provide opportunities for younger workers to voice their thoughts and suggestions about technology, which is one of their areas of true expertise and passion?*

   Do you provide an internal Facebook social network model to communicate? Does your company have its own wiki? This is one way to support their need to connect the dots about what the company does, how one department supports another, and how what they do contributes to the company. By thinking differently about how diverse the generations are, you unlock the talents of different generations eager to make even greater contributions to the team.

Millennial Minute

The intimate relationship between Millennials and technology has changed the way Millennials view work; the way they perceive their life and career. All the tech tools are part of who they are, no matter where they go. They have high expectations about their competence, as they were told they could do anything. They have been encouraged to follow their passion, even if it does not seem practical. They bring all this to the workplace, fully expecting meaningful work, flexible hours, work–life balance, and generous compensation.

✦ 6 ✦

Building RELATIONSHIPS with Gen Ys

RELATIONSHIP: the connection or the way in which two or more people or organizations regard and behave toward each other.

One of the key elements that differentiates Millennials is the expectation they have about the way work gets completed, how business relationships matter, and the environment in which the work is accomplished. Gen Ys have experienced what it feels like to work on supportive teams and how collaboration and communication enhances the process of reaching goals. Collaboration is something that Millennials are accustomed to and respond to in-kind. As this generation was matriculating through school, working on teams, collaborating was simply part of the curriculum and process by which they were educated. That, partnered with a strong dose of inclusion where everyone was included regardless of physical or personal challenges, made it so they understood their role on a team and were not shy about asking for what they needed.

Inside this collegiate type atmosphere is where this generation feels they can make the most contributions, feel appreciated, and do their best work. It could certainly be argued that everyone, regardless of their generation, would flourish under these circumstances. The difference is these younger contributors know the difference and don't feel the least bit shy in asking questions about challenging those in authority. The familiar greeting using the word "dude" as a way of saying hello is a method they apply to level the status of the relationship playing field. It doesn't matter what your title or rank, they look through the lens that we are all peers, we can all contribute at the same level.

Relationship leadership is the complete opposite of task-oriented leadership, which is focused on getting the task completed, and does not include how it might impact or affect the person doing the task. Relationship leadership is a participative style, and it encourages good teamwork and creative collaboration and supports positive behaviors. In practice, most leaders use both task-oriented and people-oriented styles of leadership.

With people-oriented leadership, leaders are totally focused on organizing, supporting, and developing the people on their teams. This includes showing appreciation for their contributions. The "command and control" style that was once so prevalent in the workplace is no longer as relevant or useful in a business environment because technologies and innovations have had a significant impact on the way business is done. Police, fire departments, emergency rooms, SWAT teams, and the military use this style successfully as emergencies and life-threatening situations require clear rules of protocol to save lives and prevent injuries. In a more day-to-day business environment with additional younger workers moving in, relationship leadership meets these employees' needs and expectations.

Being a relationship leader does not mean you will sacrifice your standards or hold anyone less accountable, but it does imply that you know the value that relationships bring to engage and motivate a team. This chapter is filled with suggestions about building effective relationships, giving and receiving appreciation, and how these, along with a relationship leadership approach, will support your ability to engage, motivate, and lead your youthful employees.

Do It R.I.G.H.T.!

The R.I.G.H.T. Model is a quick way to remember how to create an environment that fosters relationships. When built on trust, a key ingredient in engaging and leading Millennial talent, being an effective listener underscores all of the elements in the R.I.G.H.T. model. Just so you know, the reason we have two ears and only one mouth is so we can listen TWICE as often as we speak!

Characteristic	Defined As ...	Example
RESPECT	Respect is the feeling or attitude of admiration and regard towards somebody or something.	As a leader, you show your respect by: listening to your employees and valuing what they have to share; by treating everyone fairly; by being consistent in words and actions, acknowledging but not judging differences.
INTEGRITY	Integrity is the quality of possessing and adhering to high moral principles and professional standards.	Millennials have grown up in this highly connected world and expect transparency because they have the tech skills and the strong social networks that allow them to obtain information very, very quickly. They are comfortable calling out behaviors that are not consistent with the company's mission and values.
GRACE	A capacity to tolerate, accommodate, or forgive people.	Though you and your Gen Y employee completely disagreed about how to resolve a department problem that was discussed in a group meeting, you were graceful in the way you handled the situation, never embarrassing them, listening to their perspective, and maintaining their dignity.
HONESTY	Honesty is the quality or characteristic of being fair, just, truthful, and morally upright.	Though JJ is a great asset to the team, his supervisor quickly let him know that his conduct at the last team meeting was inappropriate. He shared this information one-on-one and JJ appreciated his directness and honesty. The message was real and presented in an authentic manner.
TRUST	Trust is the confidence in and reliance on fairness, truth, and honor.	Jo knew he could trust his supervisor with the information he shared in confidence and not worry about this sensitive data leaking out. Jo knows being able to trust his supervisor is one of the reasons he's so committed to his job.

Leveraging Intent to Support Effective Relationships

Intentions are something that somebody plans to do or achieve, the purpose they have in their mind. Sometimes other people misunderstand our intentions. Sometimes we misunderstand other people's intentions. Misunderstood intentions can have a serious impact on our ability to develop successful business relationships. Have you ever had the experience of trying to do something nice and the other person NOT appreciating your efforts? As a supervisor of a Gen Y, sharing your intentions is a powerful tool in explaining why you are providing feedback, coaching, or even performance correction. Intentions play an important role in effective business relationships.

In What Ways Are Intentions Communicated?

Intentions are best shared up front with clear language explaining why you are doing, sharing, or asking for something. Remember, Millennials are very good at finding information, sharing information, and working swiftly with their strong social networks. The old adage "You are on a need to know basis" does not serve this population since they will just work around you.

Letting your Millennial team know why you are doing something or asking for something is an effective tool in building strong working relationships and will probably save you time in the long run.

Intentions Are Communicated in What You Say and What You Do.

Your actions and words should be in sync so that your body language matches your message. In this tech-saturated world, anyone can record what you are saying with his or her phone or even take a picture whether or not you are aware. The vast majority of Millennials has smart phones and understands how to utilize all of the features these savvy phones provide.

What Gets in the Way of Your Ability to Communicate Your Intentions?

Intentions do not dilute your leadership or influencing capabilities. In fact, they strengthen them because when others understand why you are doing something, they can ask questions, have them answered, and then get behind the project or task at hand.

What Can Happen When Others Misunderstand Our Intentions?

People fill in the blanks when they are unclear about intentions. They assume you are doing what you are doing for your own gain and that you are not interested in helping or supporting others. Though you may not always be at liberty to share everything, explain how what is being asked fits into the scope of the work being completed or why it is important. Even though it may seem mundane, this can go a long way towards providing Millennials with the motivation they require.

✳ Case Study

Tavo is a Gen X manager who is an effective communicator and knows how to build strong business relationships. Tavo has utilized "intention setting" as the standard when beginning new projects with his team, when new people join the department, and when working with others. He has found clearly explaining what the intentions and expectations are for projects to be a great tool when directing Millennials. Here is an example:

Tavo: *"Shane, I want to talk about this new project you will be working on. It's a very high visibility project and I want to be sure you understand what's at stake."*

Shane: *"I try to do good work on all of my projects."*

Tavo: *"I know you do and that's appreciated, but this project will have a lot of people reviewing it. My intention is to be sure you understand that since so many others will be having input, we need to be very clear about why each aspect has been created and have detailed supporting documentation. Though I don't want to appear to be micromanaging, I will be checking in often, asking more questions than I usually do, and I want you to know that this will be a great learning experience as projects that have group scrutiny can be challenging. This is not about your inability to work on this project or to contribute. Please keep me well informed and if you are not clear about something, I'd appreciate being able to clarify quickly as meeting deadlines are critical."*

Shane: *"I understand and appreciate you letting me know up-front."*

Tavo: *"Great, glad you understand and I look forward to seeing some great work!"*

So What Transpired Here?

Tavo took those few minutes to share his intentions, in this case, not to undermine Shane's work because he didn't trust him, but to let him know this is a high visibility project (yes, that means political!) and must be managed accordingly. Shane won't have to mumble and grumble to his friends that his boss is being a pain; he now understands up front that this project is different and this level of detail and scrutiny is not about him.

⏱ MILLENNIAL MINUTE

The reality is that much of what Millennial workers want isn't so different from what everybody else wants, but Millennials ASK for it and feel no embarrassment for asking. Query your Millennials, engage in a conversation regularly, and find out what they are thinking. What you learn could support process improvements and maybe more efficient ways of getting work completed.

•　•　•　•　•　•　•　•　•　•　•　•　•　•　•　•　•

How Do You Repair Broken Relationships?

Repairing broken relationships is very challenging, but it can be done. The process for repairing a broken business relationship is not any different for Millennials or anyone else on your team. The difference is that Millennials need relationships to be open, honest, and transparent. When relationships have been broken, there is likely to be time spent sabotaging you, a very unproductive use of time and energy. At the very least, you owe it to yourself and the relationship to give it another try. These suggested actions provide a framework for you to put the relationship back on track.

> ➢ **Apologize.** Begin with apologizing by saying "it was my fault." Own the mistake or misunderstanding and acknowledge that what you said or the action you took was not the best way to go. Apologies must be sincere or they will not be believed.

> ➢ **Listen.** Allow the person to vent and share how he or she was feeling. Don't interrupt or try to correct by saying "but here is what happened." Just listen with your ears and body language. Once the other person has emptied their "buckets worth" of anger and frustration, he or she will more likely be able to accept your apology and move forward.

> ➢ **Ask for another chance.** The biggest push back that typically occurs is that the other person either does not believe you are truly sorry or they are concerned that it might happen again. Still, ask for another chance. Acknowledge that you know that there is a lack of trust and that trust must be earned back. Ask for the opportunity to do just that.

> ➢ **Demonstrate trust and follow-through.** Trust and following through are two of the attributes necessary for building effective business relationships. You will need to work hard at regaining trust. Consistently follow through with your words and actions to

let your Gen Y employee know that you value your business relationship and want to be back on track.

➢ **Don't justify—own the problem.** Relationships are two-way streets—it works both ways! We play a role and the other person plays a role. Though we may think they started it, that they made things worse, or they blew things out of proportion, it still takes two to have a relationship. Even though you are the "boss," you have contributed in some way to making things worse. (Be honest, you know you did!) Don't justify your behavior by telling yourself "it's okay, he or she deserves what they got." Own your part of the problem and most of the time the other will follow in kind.

Here are some ways to begin the conversation to repair a broken relationship:

"I understand your frustration and even anger. How can I help us move past this and focus on having a better relationship?"

"If there is anything you want to further discuss, I am here to listen to your point of view. "

"I know it has been uncomfortable between us and I want to clear the air. Is this a good time for us to talk?"

"Even if you don't want to speak to me, I would like to apologize for what I did. Please accept my apology, as my intentions are to clear the air and move forward."

"After calming down, I see that I over-reacted to our conversation, and would like to let you know how sorry I am that I lost my temper."

How Appreciation Supports Relationship Leadership

One prevalent perspective is that younger employees should be grateful to have a job and the opportunities associated with that position. "When I was younger I did what I was told, kept my mouth shut, and made the most of each situation." That sentiment is something we hear often from seasoned managers who just don't understand why the Millennials are not like they were when they began their careers and WHY they expect to hear "thank you" for just doing their jobs!

Millennials were raised mainly by baby boomers who often viewed their offspring as trophy kids and did everything they could to prevent their children from failing. They had a clear expectation that praise, feedback, appreciation, and kudos were part of the environment. The upside of this is a generation who think they *can*—with clear direction, daily feedback, and clear parameters—do the job you want. Ideas of appreciation do not have to include any financial costs and there are many suggestions that just take a little time and will pay big dividends.

Appreciation comes in many forms. What each manifestation has in common is an undertone of providing feedback that lets someone know what they are doing that is good and that their efforts are appreciated by you, as their boss, as well as by the organization. Here are some quick ways to provide appreciation:

1. Share what your Millennial has done on a project or an assignment that has helped the team, department, or company. These small, incremental instances of praise, accompanied by an explanation of specifically how their work has been helpful, will go a long way in keeping motivation and engagement high. Millennials want to know how what they do matters and sharing how it "fits in" to a larger context is valued.

2. Millennials have less confidence in long-term rewards and greater expectations for short-term rewards. They may perceive that the prospect for receiving long-term benefits is not secure. DO find good short-term rewards such as receiving time off, getting to select an assignment, or having flexible work hours.

3. Millennials view their professional development as part of what they do, so attending a class, workshop, or webinar is seen as growth and they appreciate the opportunity to learn and grow.

4. When your Millennial has over-delivered on a project, reward them with time off. It costs less than a monetary reward or bonus and goes far in saying you understand how important their time is to them.

5. Though you may perceive your Millennials only as employees, they probably perceive you as MORE than their supervisor. They want to share with you who they are as people, not just employees or contractors. Let them share—the more you know, the better you will be able to understand who they are, how they feel appreciated, and what motivates them.

6. Millennials started online social networks. Brainstorm ways you can leverage social networking in the workplace to encourage team collaboration and knowledge sharing. Tap into your team and listen to their input. Imagine all the great benefits that social networking can provide to your team.

(🕐) MILLENNIAL MINUTE

A large hospital chain in the Southeast United States has implemented a program to support internal promotions by providing coaching to those who apply for an internal position and do not obtain the position. This coaching process addresses readiness, specific skills, and helps demystify the "why didn't I get the job" mindset. The Gen X and Millennial employees view this as a demonstration that the company does care about their development and growth and appreciates their investment. This is a great practice!

● ● ● ● ● ● ● ● ● ● ● ● ● ● ● ● ● ● ● ●

How Millennials Show Their Appreciation: Rate My Boss!

Millennials' ability to build social online communities is a resource, the implications of which have not yet been fully felt in corporate America. Millennials have learned how to leverage technology to create communities that support their needs. For example, the site RateMyProfessors.com is dedicated to sharing who the best college teachers are, how campuses rank according to faculty, and info about why they are or are not great teachers. This site has been online since 1999 and currently offers ratings on college and university professors from over six thousand schools across the United States, Canada, England, Scotland, and Wales, with thousands of new ratings added each day. Millennials' need for information and **transparency** has become part of their DNA. If a site doesn't exist, they will create it in order to share what they know and then offer this up to their many social networking portals.

If we take the concept of rating professors and carry it to the workplace, we will have RateMyBoss! It seems a little crazy that you would be willing to supply info about good or bad bosses, but guess what? It does exist and it's called **eBossWatch.com**. This site invites you to rate your boss so that those considering a career move will have just-in-time data about the great bosses and the ones to avoid. eBossWatch was launched in June 2007 to help people avoid hostile work environments and workplace bullying. The site maintains that as it is extremely difficult during the job interview process to discover the true atmosphere at a potential employer's workplace and the true nature of a potential manager, eBossWatch aims to help by providing this information.

eBossWatch enables you to anonymously rate your boss using an evaluation form so that job seekers can search for bosses at potential workplaces and receive reports detailing the ratings that each boss received. You provide the company name and the name of the good or bad boss so others can be warned. They currently have information on the twenty-five worst bosses with names, scenarios, and the company name listed. One implication of this data is that as a company, if you don't respond quickly, it looks bad for the company's brand and as some of the scenarios listed concerned hostile workplace issues and harassment, you could now be in violation of an employee's rights.

As this data becomes so readily available, what impact will it have on performance? Will Millennials and others utilize this as they change companies and consider their opportunities? Could this type of data be the deciding factor in going to work for a company? Will some articulate Millennial say to the recruiter or hiring manager, "I really want to take this position you're offering, I think the company looks great, but I won't work for THAT boss because I know he's difficult, demanding, mean, and unfair." Maybe one of the negotiating points in the new world of work will be Millennials selecting who they will work for in the company. Will this transparency create a new dynamic in the workplace? As we continue to recover from the Great Recession and the talent market expands, what impact could the sharing of this judgmental data have on you, your team, and your company?

⏰ MILLENNIAL MINUTE

Keep the door open, but you don't need to be a doormat! Millennials appreciate a friendly, fair-minded supervisor who provides advice and support. They are not looking for pushovers, they want their supervisors to exercise their authority but still remain approachable.

The Millennials: Johnson & Johnson

Johnson & Johnson formed its first-ever generational affinity group, the Millennials, to help raise understanding of the generation and to encourage inclusion across all generations. The group serves as an educational resource and awareness advocate about Millennials' culture and characteristics, empowers and supports Millennials' professional growth and success, and works to establish relationships between Millennials and all other employees to encourage a deeper understanding of the Millennial population. The group is open for everyone—not just Millennials—to join.

Key Takeaways for Building Relationships by Understanding What Motivates Gen Y

✦ **Feeling connected.** This is a key motivator and something Millennials are accustomed to as they are "connected" via their mobile devices and through social networks in real time. Millennials bring that same need to feel connected to the workplace. Keep them as informed as possible, provide the tools and resources that can keep them "in the loop," and encourage them to share with others and make connections. One of the questions that you will be asked during an interview is what does your internal social networking look like. They want to find others who have similar interests, maybe have gone to the same schools, or belong to similar community philanthropic organizations.

✦ **Interesting work.** Okay, so it's not always interesting, but understanding how the work supports the greater good is important. For example, inputting customer comments may seem boring and a Millennial might ask why this process can't be automated. Turns out, those customer comments need to be managed and organized in a way that is useful so that what these customers are saying about the company's service can be utilized to make improvements. That can take the "sting" out of a task that seems mundane. Remember, Millennials don't come pre-wired with the "pay your dues" software!

✦ **Learning, growing, gaining experience.** Millennials are motivated to learn, grow, and experience, as that is how they have been programmed. This is not always because they want to move up, but they know that the more they know and learn, the more options they will have as they progress through their career. This becomes another opportunity for you to share why doing a task can help not just the company but them personally. They have been influenced by families and teachers/professors to believe that knowledge is the new currency.

◆ **Connection with the boss.** It has been well documented that employees of all ages leave their supervisor before they leave the company. In others words, the alignment is with the boss or supervisor much more than with the company. This is especially true at entry levels and with employees who do not have much tenure, since they have so much less to lose if they leave. Millennials are especially affected by the relationship with their boss. The good news is that when you make this relationship effective, you have a much greater chance of improving productivity and retaining talent.

◆ **Fun factor.** Yes, work is called work for a reason, but there are many things that can make the environment fun. Just ask your Millennials! (This is highlighted in TRUST in the section on Adultescents.) Asking your team how low-cost fun can be added to your environment is a great activity in proactive thinking. Provide the guidelines and parameters and see what your team comes back with—be prepared to have some fun!

⏱ MILLENNIAL MINUTE

Although work–life balance was initially demanded by Gen Xers, the sheer number of Millennials and the need for Baby Boomers to have more balance in their work life and spend their time engaged in activities they enjoy, has made this a multigenerational condition of work quality. It's clear to many Millennials that time is what they have to offer and effectively using it, not wasting it, is their mantra. Working smarter, not harder is their call to action!

✦ 7 ✦

How to Interview and ONBOARD Gen Y Talent

ONBOARD: To bring someone new to the group or the organization into the mainstream, to support the process for a new hire to fully integrate and function in their role or position. Bringing them onboard *quickly provides for a faster transition to becoming productive.*

This chapter's focus is on interviewing and onboarding Millennial talent. Since Millennials use their social networks to obtain information and continually apply that data to make decisions and move forward, even the process of interviewing Millennials has some nuances. Due to the vast amount of information that exists online as well as via social networks concerning your company and their talent, these young potential employees are able to check you and your organization out in the same way you are checking them out! They are looking for the right fit for themselves as well as looking ahead to see if your company is the type of organization they want to be a part of as they look to the near future. Also provided are questions you might *not* expect to help prepare you for different perspectives that could be new to you as you interview.

In previous generations, transitioning to a new job and not feeling comfortable, not understanding how you fit in, and not really understanding what is expected of you and where you fit into the new company environment was all a part of the process. Members of Generation Y do not see it this way and are very quick to ask for what they need and to share, good or bad, how their new job is going. Onboarding these new employees is critical to their success as well as your own. The more quickly they understand how the organization works and their role in it, the more productive they will be for you, the team, and the company.

The sections that follow are to help you interview Millennials effectively by utilizing behavior-based questions aimed at letting them talk and share. This will provide you with the opportunity to discover and learn about them, which will in turn help you determine if they would be a good fit. The great news is that they will share when asked the right questions and will be expecting you to do likewise. In addition, once you have made the hiring decision, how you bring them into the company is key to helping them become successful as quickly as possible. The passive process of learning on the job is not typically what most Millennials expect. When you have a defined process and have processes ready for them to follow, they will become engaged more quickly, feel connected, and become more productive as they onboard.

⏱ *MILLENNIAL MINUTE*

When learning about future Gen Y employees, push old assumptions aside, what you gain can have a positive and even dramatic effect!

● ● ● ● ● ● ● ● ● ● ● ● ● ● ● ● ● ● ●

Generational Messaging

Growing up, Gen Ys were bombarded with messages, more than any other generation. Due to the 24/7 nature of news and information and with their tech savvy skills and links into social media, they are connected and move forward with high expectations. The five messages we've selected also have a big impact on the interviewing and onboarding process. As you begin your preparation for interviewing, let's review these messages and look at the impact they have had on Millennial expectations. These messages have been ingrained and, as such, will come with them to the interview, possibly challenging your previous interviewing experiences!

Connected 24/7

Being so connected has many impacts on the interviewing process. To begin with, a Millennial will do her or his homework and, at the minimum, will have checked out your company's website. They will have sent a text and posted on their social network(s) that they are interviewing at your company, looking for insights, connections, and information. Once they obtain information or other connections that they believe will be useful, they will try to connect with those people so that they will have taken as close a look inside your environment as possible without actually being there.

With the research and training that I do across the country, I connect with many people at various organizations. I begin a new company project by gathering data at each company's site and I'm amazed at how many internal people do not know what is shared on their company's website! Most companies have a "career" link, which I have found to be especially useful in learning about what the company says they offer in terms of training, leadership development, and future opportunities. What is said there is what your Millennial applicants are expecting. Does what is being featured about your company's opportunities really represent the reality? (Hint: they will be asking you this during the interview.)

Be Smart—You Are Special!

They've been catered to since they were babies on a number of levels. They have been made to feel special and they have had a great deal of support and nurturing from their parents, coaches, and teachers. Brands such as Nickelodeon, Baby Gap, and Sports Illustrated for Kids were created just for this generation.

As the best-educated generation, they believe in themselves and in what they bring to a job opportunity. They view themselves as "special" and lead with confidence. They do not typically see themselves as "one of the pack," and they bring that unique quality to the interview as well as to the job.

Belief in Achievement

Millennials have been told they can do anything they want, from being president of the United States to a world class athlete. They've been told: if you focus, study, and apply yourself, you can become anything.

Since many of them have been working on their resumes and skills since childhood, and because their parents helped to provide them with meaningful experiences and traveling opportunities, they have been reared to achieve and to expect rewards for their efforts. (Millennials are not all looking for ways to become the CEO of the company, but they do want to know how the work will be meaningful and how your organization will provide educational opportunities to grow what they know and add to their body of knowledge and skills. When you have a Millennial who might be a good fit for a job opportunity, letting them know what the company provides as far as educational reimbursement or any type of learning or training and leadership program is viewed as a perk.

Community Service

Many Millennials volunteered in high school and college and bring that community service drive with them on an interview. They want to know how your company supports the surrounding communities and/or how you help others through philanthropic endeavors.

This perspective is a great thing on the job. How you apply this to your organization creates a win-win. Millennials want to give back and when they have an opportunity to do that on the job, they perceive it as a perk.

Millennials' Values

Millennials are inclusive and tolerant of others' races, religions, cultures, and sexual orientation. Millennials have an inclusive dimension and have a greater sensitivity to attitudes pertaining to race, religion, culture, or sexual orientation that they feel might not be appropriate.

Much has been written about their strong tech skills, their expectation that their world can be customized, and their ability to connect or create social networks. Consider these strong qualities to see how they can add value and improve your work environment.

How do these messages impact the interviewing experience? Millennials are looking for a glimpse into your company and what it would be like to work for you and your brand. They bring the idea that work can be fun, and that working efficiently is the way to go. Work–life balance is at the forefront of their minds and as the most educated generation, one third of them have college degrees (and many plan to continue their education), they understand the benefits knowledge can bring to the workplace and their marketability.

Many Gen Ys have been told that they should follow their "passion" and have gone to school and traveled in search of those passions. They have been encouraged and coached to follow their dreams, knowing that their families will be standing by supportively. With this level of support, fortunate Millennials have been afforded many choices. Often they are welcome to remain at home until they are ready to move out. Since many have strong and effective relationships with their families, living at home well into your twenties does not have the same social negativity as previous generations who married younger.

⏱ MILLENNIAL MINUTE

As Millennials are accustomed to collaborating, having worked together in groups at school, they see their parents and peers as colleagues. Use that as a vehicle to bring these new hires into the company more quickly. Connect them with people in the organization, whether they directly relate to their work or not. They have the tools and skills to learn from others once provided the opportunity to do so.

● ● ● ● ● ● ● ● ● ● ● ● ● ● ● ● ● ● ● ●

Questions You Wouldn't Expect During an Interview with Gen Ys

Millennials bring their sense of transparency to the interview—they believe transparency should work both ways. Though they are the interviewees, their mindset is that they, too, need to ask questions that will allow them to peer into your corporate culture and discover what working for your company would really be like on a daily basis.

So don't be surprised if you experience the following questions during an interview. It's better to be prepared than to be shocked!

If I don't like my boss, how can I get that changed?

Millennials are accustomed to having others move the pieces of their chessboard around because their Helicopter Parents moved obstacles out of the way, coached the coaches, called the school, and advocated about all things that impacted their children. They have seen this behavior modeled and are doing what they've witnessed by expecting someone else will help them with this

How many hours per day will I be expected to work?

Yes, they are asking you how much time they will need to put in to do the job. Millennials do have work ethic, they just know that they are efficient and can get things done more quickly than people from other generations. Working remotely with clear guidelines about what they need to accomplish and deliver can be a win-win for this employee and your company.

Do you allow the use of Facebook?

Growing up with blurred boundaries is a part of the Millennials experience. They do not see the division of work and leisure—it all blends together as they multitask their way down the list. Checking in on Facebook seems as natural to them as checking your voicemail might seem to you. Many Millennials come "pre-wired" as their phones can now access any website, any time they want.

If I don't like my pay, who do I talk to about fixing that?

At the heart of this comment is the echo of the intense focus parents had on ensuring their Millennial children were treated with dignity and respect. They were allowed to be leaders and in their families, thereby preserving and enhancing their self-esteem and feelings of importance. This is where the idea originated that in sporting events EVERYONE should get a trophy, even for just showing up, so that no one's feelings would get hurt.

Millennials ask for what they want and do not understand why someone wouldn't. Setting clear parameters and guidelines here is a good way to go. What is your company's policy about pay increases? If it is a merit-based system and they want to excel, what does exceeding job expectations look like and sound like on a daily basis?

If we do reading for work, can we do it at the gym during work hours?

Multitasking is a cornerstone of their experience growing up in a busy, digital world. Doing multiple things at the same time is how they managed. Millennials have been taught to look for the most efficient ways to operate and, as a result, have found themselves working with an increasingly faint line separating work and play. Though you may be somewhat shocked when you think about this question, your thoughts centered on the disbelief caused by being asked this, it is important to consider it within the perspective of this new mindset. If you think about it in this way, it does have some value!

Who will be my mentor and coach while I'm learning to execute the tasks necessary for this job?

Millennials are accustomed to a lot of attention and to understanding how they will become proficient at the new tasks or skills required of them. At school the teachers and professors provide a rubric. In many cases rubrics are provided to students at the time an assignment is given so they know exactly what to do to achieve a certain grade. Most Millennials are used to well-defined assign-ments, clear benchmarks, and continual feedback and discussion. As such, it is a process they assume will also be in place in the busi-ness world.

What does the company do to make work fun?

Millennials don't bring the mindset that the reason it's called "work" is because it is work! They read about the "cool compa-nies" which offer yoga, movie nights, coffee bars, basketball courts, and free, on-site lunches. Making work fun is possible, but requires a new paradigm.

Millennials are not disrespecting the relationship between employer and employee; they just do not see it in the traditional way you, as the recruiter or hiring manager, may perceive. Standing in Millennial shoes and understanding why they think the way they do and what their experiences have been that have caused them to bring these questions to an interview, will provide you with a great deal of insight. Deciding that you will not inter-view anyone who has personal data about themselves on their resume, such as the type of yoga they prefer or their favorite kind of music, will significantly limit the talent pool from which you can select.

About Those Millennial Resumes . . .

In my work around the country talking to a variety of leaders, one of the comments I often get is: why is there so much personal information on the younger generation's resumes? Why do these Millennials feel so compelled to share? Do I really *need* to know about their exercise rou-tine or that they are vegan? Rather than resist, think about this as an opportunity to learn more about this person. The more you know, the better you will have an idea of how they will match the skills needed for the job, as well as if their attributes and characteristics will be a good match for the team. Without having to probe, they are offering infor-mation. It's a gift—take it as such!

⏰ MILLENNIAL MINUTE

Consistent with previous studies, Millennials place a higher premium on the success of their personal lives than on their careers. But there is more to this story. They want to spend time with their families and fulfill career aspirations. Sixty-five percent of respondents say that being successful in a high-paying career or profession is either one of the most important things in their lives or very important. They have not rejected the corporate world. More than 72 percent say they are interested in working in a big corporation someday, with 48 percent saying that their ideal career path would be working at only one or two companies over the course of their careers.[21]

• • • • • • • • • • • • • • • • • •

Interviewing Questions for Millennial Talent

As you look for skills, qualities and attributes, and begin to assess whether this candidate will be a good fit for the department and the company, let's take a look at the interviewing process.

As we've reviewed, Millennials come to the interview with a different set of experiences than other generations, but they also tend to be open and honest (remember how important transparency is to their worldview) and this can be utilized in your favor.

Interviews utilizing behavioral-based questions is a process many companies practice. Specific behavioral-based questions during interviewing are used for discovering how the interviewee acted in specific employment-related situations. The reasoning is that how you behaved in the past will predict how you will behave in the future, i.e., past performance predicts future performance.

In a traditional interview, you will be asked a series of questions which typically have straightforward answers like: "What are your strengths and weaknesses?" or "What major challenges and problems did you face? How did you handle them?" or "Describe a typical work week."

In an interview based on these kinds of queries, an employer has decided what skills are needed in the person they hire and will ask questions to find out if the candidate has those skills. Instead of asking how you would behave, they will ask how you did behave. The interviewer will want to know how you handled a situation instead of what you might do in the future. Behavioral-based interview questions will be more pointed, probing, and specific than traditional interview questions.

Interviewing Questions in a Behavioral-Based Interview Focused on Millennials

The following chart shows questions that are focused on the person who is interviewing for a position as an individual contributor.

Questions	How this helps
1. Provide an example of a time when you used logic to solve a problem.	This can be insightful as it starts to show you how they think and what processes they believe are logical.
2. Share an example of a goal you reached and how you achieved it.	What goal did they pick? What does this goal say about this person? How does their idea of a goal connect with your idea of a meaningful goal?
3. Share an example of when you went above and beyond the call of duty?	What does this example say about them? If their response expresses a willingness to help others, this might positively impact how they will play on the team and is a great indicators of how they will perform on the job.
4. How have you handled a difficult situation with a coworker? With a boss?	Understanding how someone handles a difficult situation with both a coworker and a boss will help you determine if their method of solving problems will mesh with your company's culture.
5. Share an example of how you worked effectively under pressure.	What happens when pressure is on? Because of the transparent nature of most Millennials, they will share with you what this looks like and you will be able to determine if the amount of pressure they can handle will fit with the amount of pressure that occurs in your department and your company.
6. When working on multiple projects, how did you prioritize?	How does this candidate determine what comes first and what comes second? Understanding their thought process can provide great insight
7. How did you handle meeting a tight deadline?	This provides some insight into how they work under deadline pressure. This is especially important if deadline pressure is a constant part of your work environment.
8. How do you manage your schedule when it is interrupted?	This can begin the conversation about how this candidate interacts with others and can help you see how flexible they perceive themselves to be.
9. Share an example of how you set goals and achieved them.	What type of goals did they share? What was their strategy for accomplishing goals?
10. What do you do if you disagree with your boss?	This could provide insight into this candidate's diplomacy and tact.
11. Provide an example of how you worked on a team, your role, and how you worked alongside coworkers.	Learning about how a candidate perceives their role on their team and how they interact with their peers and coworkers can provide a great deal of insight into how they handle situations at work.

Questions	How this helps
Questions for Millennial candidates who will supervise others	
1. Describe a decision you made that was unpopular and how you handled implementing it.	This can lead to an interesting discussion about boundaries, standing up for what they believe to be "right," and understanding how to maneuver inside of a political situation.
2. Did you ever make a risky decision? Why? How did you handle it?	What does this candidate gauge is a risky decision? How they handled it will provide insight into how they think.
3. Share an example of how you were able to motivate employees or coworkers.	Learning how the candidate motivates their team and coworkers provides a look into their supervision style and gives you a specific illustration of what motivation means to them.
4. How have you handled a difficult situation with another department?	Managing conflict is tricky—discovering how they navigate will be helpful in determining how they might handle a political scenario and also as you assess if this candidate would be the right fit for the position.

Follow-up questions for an interview can also be detailed as you press for more information and specifics. Try using the following:

Tell me more about that ...

"Why did you opt to go in that direction?"

"What did you learn from that situation?"

"What would you have done differently?"

"Why did you find that challenging?"

"If you had an opportunity for a "do-over," what would you change?"

"How did that make you feel?"

"How did you react when "XYZ" occurred?"

Note: These questions can be used with any candidate; the beauty is when you ask these behavioral-based questions, Millennials will share information without as much hesitation as people with more work experience from different generations.

The goal of an effective interview based on these behavioral-based questions is to allow the candidate to share their experiences and for you to have that view into their past and determine if they would be a good hire and fit for your current opening. The more conversational and less formal you can structure the interview, the more at ease the candidate will feel and the more information you will obtain. A good rule of thumb to really get to know the candidate is to have them speaking 80 percent of the time and you 20 percent. When you put the candidate at ease, listen more than you speak and encourage the candidate to talk, they will tell you a lot!

Onboarding Gen Y New Hires

In chapter one, we outlined the importance of a rubric to help Millennial talent understand how to get an "A" and what it takes to be successful as you and the company define what is expected. When you are onboarding a new Millennial to your team, he or she is looking for the roadmap of how the company works, what's expected, how to find resources, and who to go to with questions.

A company handbook that contains the rules of employment is critical, but these documents do not provide all that is needed. These handbooks are often referred to as the "rules of the road" and must be reviewed and signed off, thereby indicating that the employee understands these rules and agrees to comply. What these handbooks don't provide is the information about the company's culture, which speaks to things like expectations of how we should behave when a client is onsite, or if you are going to make microwave popcorn you need to take it to the break-room at the back of the building, or that "casual Friday" is only okay on Saturday! (Think about it—there are companies that have not embraced casual Friday and it's important that all of these cultural nuances are shared and communicated.)

They will appreciate your being strong and clear, and stating that your intentions are to make new employees successful because their success is your success. Then share how you like to receive communication how often department or team meetings occur, and tell them that being on time is critical. Inform them that you are giving them examples of what is expected and this will likely also be covered in the rule book.

Creating an Onboarding RoadMap

You may be fortunate enough to work for an organization that has a well-developed "onboarding" program and process for new hires. If they do not, then here are some guidelines as you create your own roadmap. Like any good map, it can only provide guidance—it is not a substitute for being able to ask questions or seek clarification. Effective onboarding answers the following questions:

"What does the company/organization do? What is the company's history? What is unique about the company?"

"What is the company's/organization's mission? What are the values and/or guiding principles? How do these principles apply to the new hire, and what is their expectation regarding my behavior?"

"What are the business indicators that guide our business direction—sales results, customer satisfaction, reports, etc."

"How do I connect with others on the team, in other departments or other divisions?"

"What is my job, day-to-day? (Providing a "Day in the Life" scenario would be helpful as you paint a picture and begin providing job expectations and parameters.)"

"What is the rubric for this employee's position?"

"How will performance be measured?"

"Who can I go to with questions?"

"How do I connect with others through the intranet?"

"How do I learn about career opportunities?"

⏱ MILLENNIAL MINUTE

Ask your newest team members to make a list of all the things they did not understand when they joined the company. This list will provide great insight into the "things not covered" as they learn about the rules of the road, as well as provide a great outline for what new people joining the team will need to know. Putting this in the form of a "wiki" (online or hard copy) in the spirit of Wikipedia will be familiar to your younger staff and effective for everyone!

●   ●   ●   ●   ●   ●   ●   ●   ●   ●   ●   ●   ●   ●   ●   ●   ●   ●

Global New Directions: General Electric

To help transition its Millennial workforce to GE's culture, HR leaders at GE formed a team of twenty-one Millennials from various GE businesses and functions with a goal to identify ways to attract, develop, and retain Millennial talent. The team, named "Global New Directions," returned from their three-month assignment with the following recommendations that were adopted by senior leaders:

- Use gaming technology to connect the world to GE in a fun and engaging way to educate prospective employees about the company's values.

- Create a personalized suite of benefits that offers more flexibility and choice to better meet the needs of GE's global, diverse workforce.

- Enhance performance management systems with new tools to help employees navigate their careers at GE, to identify a wider range of job opportunities throughout the company, and to offer more "just-in-time" feedback and coaching.[22]

Key Takeaways for Embracing Discovery: The Importance of Being Gen Y-Friendly

Educating managers and supervisors to engage with Gen Y in their comfort zone is critical to avoid high turnover and the indifference that often occurs when a workplace is not Millennial-friendly. Unlike other groups of workers, this demographic has no loyalty and harbors deep skepticism about the business world—that is, until they come to appreciate and trust their supervisors. Research clearly indicates that Millennials do not have a strong alliance to organizations. However, they can form very strong bonds with their supervisors, which is where so much of the important work occurs.

Daniel W. Rasmus, author of the books *Listening to the Future* and *Management by Design* and sought-after speaker on the impact of Generation Y in the workplace said:

> My research suggests that Millennials remain very cynical about the corporations in which they work. They have heard about outsourcing, downsizing, and layoffs for years. According to the data

I've seen, they were laid off in greater numbers than older workers during the recession, which reinforced their lack of trust or any motivation to create a lasting relationship with any firm. If individual organizations want to regain the trust of this generation, they need to go to extraordinaire measures and be willing to make the investments, like mentoring, training, and investing in company social networks, and other measures, that will help prove they are worthy places for these young people to place their loyalty.

We can either look at age warfare as the Millennials and Boomers battle it out for dominance in the workplace, or we can negotiate a mutually beneficial common ground that will engage employees and help organizations innovate.

Ultimately this is a business continuity issue, and thus a strategic issue, for most organizations. They don't have a real choice in confronting it. If they make the choice of ignoring the issue, it will be a strategic misstep. If they embrace it, they may well find it a competitive advantage, especially if they do it sooner than later.

The Future of Generation Y

Through the research and work I've done as well as the work in collaboration with other professionals, I continue to have enormous optimism about the Millennial Generation! These young people come to the workplace with so much to share, wanting to partner and contribute in the unique, collaborative (you're my peer) style that they are accustomed to and that has been so successful in their lives so far.

Though diversity awareness has been a part of organizational culture for many years, now generational diversity—the wide breadth of ages in today's workforce—is becoming an area of strategic opportunity for organizations of all sizes. When looking at an organization through the lens of those born in different decades, it becomes clear that all bring different ideas, expectations, work habits, and experience to the job. Getting managers to understand and appreciate those differences can help companies maximize the talents of each demographic. It's a natural process, to at first resist that which is not familiar, but in the case of so many Millennials entering the workplace, resisting is the worst possible strategy. Increasingly, progressive companies are launching enterprise-wide initiatives to address generational diversity because the age range in today's workforce is unprecedented.

My colleague Daniel W. Rasmus, also shared the following in his blog http://danielwrasmus.com/welcome-to-the-serendipity-economy/:

In my paper, "Welcome to the Serendipity Economy," I suggest that a parallel economy exists, and has existed, alongside our industrial economy, one that is unpredictable in both the value it produces and the time it takes for that value to be realized. And it is an economy that cannot be modeled because it reconfigures itself constantly, staying just out of reach of those attempting to quantify it.

I think the Millennials are uniquely qualified to leverage this parallel economy. They network globally and are willing to explore unconventional means of employment, as well as to challenge underlying assumptions. What will this mean for the workplace? I think it may well mean a continued deterioration of the traditional workplace, the single, coordinated organization where employment and inclusion are synonymous. The Millennials, again serendipitously, are facing a post-recession world where temporary work through contract agencies has played a big role in job creation. Uncertainty at all levels means that companies aren't willing to risk full-time employment when roles can be adequately filled by contract employees who are much more expendable and, perhaps more importantly, reconfigurable as the economy ebbs and flows and technology and business practice change underlying assumptions. ...

As the baby boomers retire in the years to come and the size of Gen Xers in the workforce also decreases as they take time out to raise their children, Millennials will be called upon to fill in the labor gaps. Manager training programs that anticipate Millennials' inherently different workplace expectations are the ones likely to build productive teams and create new leaders. In short, new times require new tactics. Companies that rethink their approach to training and developing younger workers are likely to gain a significant advantage. Investing in this talented generation is an investment in your departments as well as your company's and country's future. By 2014 Millennials will be 47 percent of the workforce—are you ready?

> "We don't see things as they are; we see things as we are."
> —Anaïs Nin, writer

Notes

1. Rob Salkowitz, *Generation Blend Managing Across the Technology Age Gap* (New York: John Wiley & Sons, Inc. 2008), 3.

2. Jessica Brack, "Maximizing Millennials in the Workplace," UNC Kenan-Flagler Business School, accessed August 1, 2012, http://www.kenan-flagler.unc.edu/executive-development/custom-programs/~/media/DF1C11C056874DDA8097271A1ED48662.ashx.

3. Rebecca Leung, "60 Minutes: The Echo Boomers," CBS News, February 11, 2009, http://www.cbsnews.com/stories/2004/10/01/60minutes/main646890.shtml.

4. Millennial Online Survey Research, The End Result Partnerships Inc., March 2010.

5. "52%—For Millennials, Parenthood Trumps Marriage," Pew Research Center, http://pewresearch.org/databank/dailynumber/?Number ID=1522.

6. Graeme Codrington, "Adultescence—the New Young Adult," *Tomorrow Today*, February 18, 2006, http://connectioneconomy.com/2006/02/18/adultescence-the-new-young-adult/.

7. "Interesting Tattoo Fact: Millennials Are by Far the Most Tattooed Generation," *Tania Marie' Blog: Creating Life as a Work of Art*, last modified March 29, 2012, http://taniamarieartist.wordpress.com/2012/03/29/interesting-tattoo-fact-millennials-are-by-far-the-most-tattooed-generation/.

8. http://www.diversityinc.com/resource-groups-2/do-you-need-a-generational-employee-resource-group/.

9. Paul J. Zak, "The Neurobiology of Trust," *Scientific American* (May 19, 2008).

10. Susan Adams, "Employee Loyalty Dropping Worldwide," *Forbes*, (November 10, 2011), accessed August 1, 2012, http://www.forbes.com/sites/susanadams/2011/11/10/employee-loyalty-dropping-worldwide/.

11. Randstad 2008 World of Work survey, http://us.randstad.com/content/aboutrandstad/knowledge-center/employer-resources/World-of-Work-2008.pdf.

12. Cali Ressler and Jody Thompson, *Why Work Sucks and How to Fix It: No Schedules, No Meetings, No Joke—the Simple Change That Can Make Your Job Terrific* (New York: Penguin Group, 2008).

13. Nick Shore, "Millennials Are Playing with You," *Harvard Business Review,* (December 12, 2011), http://blogs.hbr.org/cs/2011/12/millennials_are_playing_with_y.html.

14. Ferris Jabr, "The Neuroscience of 20-Somethings," *Scientific American* (August 29, 2012), http://blogs.scientificamerican.com/brainwaves/2012/08/29/the-neuroscience-of-twenty-somethings.

15. http:Omaha.com/index.php?u page=1219&u_sid=10077175.

16. Christopher Noxon, *Rejuvenile: Kickball, Cartoons, Cupcakes, and the Reinvention of the American Grown-up* (New York: Three Rivers Press, 2006).

17. Mark McCrindle, "New Generations at Work: Attracting, Recruiting, Retraining & Training Generation Y," McCrindle Research, 2006, http://www.scribd.com/doc/12310739/New-Generations-at-Work.

18. Lauren Stiller Rikleen, "Creating Tomorrow's Leaders: The Expanding Roles of Millennials in the Workplace," Boston College Center for Work & Family, 2011.

19. Sylvia Ann Hewlett, Laura Sherbin, and Karen Sumberg, "How Gen Y & Boomers Will Reshape Your Agenda," *Harvard Business Review,* (July–August 2009).

20. Cara Pring, "99 New Social Media Stats for 2012," *The Social Skinny,* (May 10, 2012), http://thesocialskinny.com/99-new-social-media-stats-for-2012/.

21. "Millennials and the Corporate World," Bentley University, Center for Women & Business, http://www.bentley.edu/centers/center-for-women-and-business/millennials-and-corporate-world.

22. Susan Peters, "How GE Is Attracting, Developing, and Retaining Global Talent," *Harvard Business Review,* (February 8, 2012), http://blogs.hbr.org/cs/2012/02/how_ge_is_attracting_and_devel.html.

About the Author

Diane Spiegel is a founding partner of The End Result Partnerships Inc. and is one of the nation's recognized leaders in corporate training and development. With more than twenty-five years of experience, Diane is an industry leader and innovator who created the firm's highly successful training methodology, Sage Leadership Tools. An organizational architect, Diane specializes in developing training plans that offer companies a strategic process to educate and develop their employees and provide the framework for cultural and organizational change.

Diane has authored and designed many leadership and supervisory training programs for Fortune 1000 companies that have increased companies' talent promotion rates, decreased company turnover and improved employee engagement. Diane earned a Bachelor of Arts degree in sociology and psychology from California State University, Fullerton, and she completed post-graduate study in employee relations and organizational development at the University of California, Irvine. She is certified in MBTI and PULSE POINT.

Diane's clients include Azamara Cruises, Celebrity Cruises, Corinthian Colleges, Costco, Del Taco International, Southern California Edison, Jamba Juice, Legoland California, MRL Reference Laboratory, Option One Mortgage, Royal Caribbean International, Shutterfly, South Coast Plaza Management, Sunglass Hut/Watch Station, The Gap, The Limited, 3M, Wet Seal, and Wolfgang Puck Cafes.

Diane is a featured blogger on the American Express OPEN website as an expert (Managing category) on Millennials. (http://www. open forum.com/articles/why-hiring-millennials-is-good-for-your-business & http://www.openforum.com/articles/5-coaching-suggestions-for-engaging-millennials) Diane has written articles about Millennials for *PIHRA*

Magazine as well as their online site, for *Cruise Industry News*, *QSR Magazine* (Quick Service Restaurants), Nursing Advance website, Tech Flash blog, and she maintains a blog site about engaging and leading Millennials in today's workplace.

Diane has been a featured speaker at ASTD, PIHRA, C.H.A.R.T. and IABC and other business associations and is currently adjunct faculty at University California, Irvine, providing professional development in the area of managing the multi-generations in the workplace with an emphasis on communicating with Millennials.